Biting
the
Bullet

Essays on the Courage of Women

Biting
the
Bullet

Essays on the Courage of Women

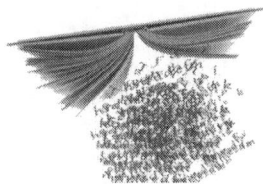

Chatter House Press
Indianapolis, IN

Biting the Bullet
Essays on the Courage of Women

Cover design by Kelsey Dunning

For information:

Chatter House Press
7915 S Emerson Ave, Ste B303
Indianapolis, IN 46237

chatterhousepress.com

ISBN: 978-1-937793-34-0

Dedication

To women of all ages
striving to live
honestly and forcefully
day-to-day

Also by Chatter House Press

Banking the Bacon
Essays on the Success of Women
Penny Dunning, editor

Let Them Eat Moon Pie®
The Southern Fried Poetry Slam From 1992 - 2000
by Bill Abbott

Written in the Dish Pit
by Adam Henze

Gems from the Bargain Bin
by Lisa Devon

Warren Avenue
by Nancy Pulley

Where in the World We Meet
by Todd Outcalt

The Mother Poems
A Memoir: The Warrior Queen Novelist
and Her Poet Daughter
by Liza Hyatt

Company of Women: New & Selected Poems
Jayne Marek, Lylanne Musselman, & Mary Sexson

Almost Music from Between Places
by Stephen R. Roberts

Samadhipada: Word Yoga
by Helen Townsend

Table of Contents

1st Place
Barbara A Barton
Michigan

Barbara Barton is an Associate Professor of Social Work at Western Michigan University where she principally teaches Leadership and Organizational Development courses at the Master's-level. She has been in the rehabilitation and brain injury fields as a clinician and an Administrator for over 20 years. She is a proud Michigan State Spartan with a number of service and teaching awards.

She is honored to share her life experiences in refreshing ways and hopes that her readers can identify a piece of themselves in her writing. In her spare time, she enjoys writing, serious bargain shopping, and theatre. Her blog address is barbara.barton@weebly.com. She is a Detroit native, but has lived in various cities in the Midwest and believes you "...bloom where you're planted."

Barbara A Barton

Words from a Warrior

A KNOTTED ROPE LAYS
SPIRALED ON THE GROUND, BEGGING
HER TO JUST. GIVE. UP.

This Haiku describes how I felt as I played with a neighbor kid's jump rope, which I had fashioned into a noose, the day after I found out I had Multiple Sclerosis.

I wanted it to be the roller coasters. Roller coasters and my increasing age. Roller coasters and the too tight pressure of the lap bar. Roller coasters that looped and yanked my body into unnatural positions.

My feet had been numb for three days, so I spent the weekend following a trip to Cedar Point Amusement Park in Ohio with my 28 year-old feet propped and elevated, in between trips to the medicine cabinet for more ibuprofen. I must have pinched a nerve, I thought

I finally agreed with my mother that I needed to make a doctor's appointment on Monday. My primary care doctor agreed to see me Monday afternoon.

"Jim, I am getting too old to ride goddamn roller coasters," I began the recanting of my weekend to my friend-- and my physician. "Both feet have permanently fallen asleep and the feeling is slowly creeping higher. Maybe its varicose veins. Do varicose veins cause you to have numb sensations? Or bunions. My grandma had bunions. Could I be growing some bunions?" There was a bevy of diagnoses I feared, so I skirted over them by bringing up bunions and veins.

"Let's get you set up with a neurologist and some testing." I walked like a gosling behind my physician as he sprinted out of the examination room, in search of a phone. *I always suck at tests* was my first thought. But I listened as he made a number of phone calls, and in twenty minutes I had an MRI scheduled as well as an appointment with a neurologist.

I walked, covered in very little hospital-issued fabric, to the MRI machine. My physician didn't buy my argument for sprouting bunions, or bulging veins. In fact, he put a name to those diagnoses I most feared, to prepare me for what these weird sensations might be:

My MRI was scheduled in 45 minutes. I waited in a very thin, hospital-issued garment for my name to be called in the Radiology department. My name was called. A bubbly young woman escorted me back to the giant, metal, cave.

I took one look at the MRI machine and panicked: "There is NO WAY my ass is going to fit in that tiny tube!" I said to a technician, louder than what was politely appropriate. I was 280 pounds and the slim body tray looked like it was a piece of a thong I possessed.

"I doubt you weigh more than 400 pounds, and that's what these machines were designed to accommodate," reassured the technician. I sat on the sliding tray and laid on my back. The technician placed a heavy, plastic mask over my head, effectively locking it in place so that it could not move. I was covered with a blanket, and another hospital worker grabbed my arm and announced: "This is the contrast dye," as she found a vein for the IV.

Contrast dye? I didn't know what was being contrasted. I was quickly becoming claustrophobic even before I was pushed into the tube that I was sure was too small for my hips.

I felt myself being propelled horizontally in the direction of my helmeted head. I immediately started to hyperventilate. Just as I was about to try to kick my way out of the tube, I was pulled out of the trap.

"All done!" chirped the technician. "We only had to repeat one series because you had moved." *Was there a Wall of Fame somewhere that contained the names of those of us who only moved once during the MRI scan?*

I was helped off the table and escorted to the changing room. Once in my clothes, the gravity of the possibilities stunned me:

Multiple sclerosis: incurable.

Guillain-Barre': could be on a respirator soon.

Amyotrophic Lateral Sclerosis: a slow death.

The diagnoses played like a film reel in my head as I drove back to the hospital where I worked in Fund Development. I was cultivating the relationship with a potential million dollar donor, with whom I was to have lunch.

I popped into our Administrative Assistant's office to tell her I was going to meet The Donor. Her phone rang, and it turned out it was my line.

"You wanna take it?" Sherry said to me.

"Yeah, I better in case something came up with The Donor."

I put her phone to my ear and I was surprised to hear my neurologist's voice.

"Yes, Barb. This is Dr. Ballard."

"Hi, Dr. Ballard. *Pleaseletitbegoodnewspleaseletitbegoodnews. Why did he call me directly?*

I glanced at my watch. I was going to be late.

"I'm afraid I have bad news. We found a lesion on your brain."

Ah-ha! Brain cancer! Another curable option.

"So what's the plan? Can we surgically remove it?" I tried to appear knowledgeable, having just gone through the brain cancer battle with my deceased fiancé.

"It's actually not operable. I regret to tell you that you have multiple sclerosis. The lesion is consistent with that profile. The lesion is located in one of the ventricles of your brain. We also found a lesion at T-11 in your spinal cord." He sounded like this was the worst part of his job. I'm sure it was. "Can you come in tomorrow at 11:00 a.m."

I really couldn't, but this would turn out to be one of the many times I moved aside my life to make room for MS.

I was still standing in my Assistant's office, but now I grabbed the edge of the desk. I did not want MS. *Incurable. No treatments. A very 'pitying' disease. No one with MS I ever saw looked happy.*

"Sherry. Can you please call the restaurant and apologize to The Donor for my sudden emergency and tell him I'll reschedule our lunch? And please cancel everything on my calendar for this afternoon." I lurched out of her office and willed my right ankle not to buckle. It held my weight as I made the short walk to my office. I grabbed the purse that cost me nearly a full paycheck, shut off the computer, and walked past the half dozen people whose eyes were on me. It felt like 600 eyeballs trying to figure out what I was thinking.

I jabbed the elevator button and looked at no one on my floor as I made the turn in the elevator. I hit the 11th floor button. *Why am I going up?* The door opened on the 11th floor, and I was pushing the elevator panel with both hands:

1st Floor, Lobby, Door Open, Door Close. *Oh my God. Get to the car. Get to the car.* After a couple of stops I landed in the Lobby.

The walk to the supersize parking lot seemed to take hours. I walked slowly, though it felt like my body was about to climax. My blood was pumping hard, my heart was beating harder. Hands, legs, and arms tingled with anticipation.

I passed my car three times before it could grab my attention. I unlocked the door and sat lightly down on the driver's seat. I had to manually lift my legs. I forgot how weak they had become. The ignition and engine churned twice before the car started and the obscenely loud CD I had been playing crushed me. The CD was Melissa Etheridge singing about how she used to love to dance. *Goddamn it! Why that song now? I was a dancer, a choreographer, a director, an opera singer. I was. I was. I was...*

I quickly popped the CD out and locked the car doors. I was preparing to surrender to my body. I was sweating. Whatever feeling I was about to experience was visceral. I closed my eyes and grabbed the gray steering wheel. My chest relaxed into the boundless energy of the breaths I took. *Inhale. Exhale. Inhale. Exhale. Let it out. Out. It has to come out!*

I lit a cigarette and set it in the red Topaz' ashtray.

I leaned back into the seat and the climax emerged with urgency in the form of a scream in the low baritone voice range. It hurt my throat. It was a pain I welcomed: it meant I was still alive. I could not stop screaming. I seamlessly took breaths as I needed to. The pitch was consistent. I started to cry, which raised the pitch of the wail slightly. I let the sound roll out of my body and the mucous flowed from my nose onto my blazer. My hands seemed to get energy from the steering wheel, so I gripped it tighter. I screamed a steady stream of vowels that seemed to have no meaning, but which contained everything I was feeling.

I do not know how long I was screaming, but I looked down and saw a long stream of ash running up the length of the ashtray, silenced by the filter.

I relied on motor and muscle memory to get home. I walked unevenly up the flight of stairs to my bedroom. Buttons popped, and zippers separated as I tugged the clothes off my damaged body and broken brain. I set the alarm for 6 a.m., laid on top of the homemade quilt, and let my pillow drown me.

I knew more than the average person about what the possibilities were, after nearly ten years of administrative and clinical social work in medical settings. I envisioned myself talking to my neurologist. I was afraid that when he opens his mouth I was about to be damned.

How do The Damned act? How do they look? Who decides who's damned and who's not? MS. No treatment yet. It seems some people are damned and the disease ravages them, while others are not so damned. They can pass as Normal People most of the time

It took two laps around a busy traffic island before I found his office. I waited in the contemporarily- decorated waiting room in a mauve, upholstered chair. I almost sat in the blue one, but the mauve chair matched my outfit better. I picked up a pamphlet on epilepsy and intently read it, trying to concentrate. There were pamphlets on MS on the tables, but I did not, could not, pick one of those up. Much better to have a seizure disorder. It was more visible to others when your sickness strikes. There are pills for epilepsy. There were no pills for MS.

A door that separated the holding tank from the examination rooms opened:

"Barbara B.," a nurse loudly intoned. *Oh my God. Why am I the one who is the patient when you, Loud Nurse, clearly need a makeover?*

I pretended I was the mother of a sick child. I was dressed better than anybody else in the waiting room. I clutched the epilepsy pamphlet as if it contained news about my child. I walked slowly to make sure I wouldn't fall. I looked Normal.

I followed her to an examination room. In less than five minutes my tall neurologist entered and towered over me with my file and some MS pamphlets. *I don't want those fucking pamphlets. I do not want you towering over me. I do not want you to speak. I do not want to stare at the creases in your white coat.* I stood up and leaned against the wall to the right of the chair in which I had sat. The neurologist now towered only a scant foot over me. The neurologist warmly greeted me, and called me Ms. Barton. I smiled a gentle smile, told him to call me Barb, and greeted him back: a model patient in control of her emotions.

"I know how hard it's going to be for you to come to terms with this all at once. I deal with it every day, and everyone's different." With that, the first MS salvo was thrown by my neurologist.

"Let's first talk about multiple sclerosis," the neurologist droned.

I heard the full report from my neurologist about multiple sclerosis with emotional numbness. I did not cry. I did not scream. I didn't yell at the neurologist that the test result belonged to someone else, and that all I needed was a vacation and good sex. All I heard, that hit me with the force of a kickball aimed at my head, was one phrase that turned into a loud echo that drowned out any other noise in the entire block:

"Prepare yourself for significant disability."

Oh my God. Oh my God. Oh my God. Annette Funicello: wheelchair. Richard Pryor: wheelchair. How do you work a wheelchair? There's steps everywhere. How would I drive, cook, walk my dogs, go antiquing? NONONONONONONONONO NONOOONONONONO. I do not want this. Take those words back right now. "Prepare yourself for significant disability," my neurologist pronounced. What does he mean by "significant"? I have something bad that is "significant." I never heard a doctor say that before.

We looked at my MRI scan together and I saw what MS looks like: illuminated white spots on my brain and spinal cord that were going to breed and hijack my body. Then he said, "I'm sorry," as if he took the doughnut I was going to reach for, or a cab that we were both trying to hail, that stopped in front of him. He gently circled my elbow with his hand and escorted me out of his office. It was a Friday. The day of the week, I found out from a nurse later, for the "chronics."

I was now a chalkboard for people to write the words that describe me:

A "chronic."

Disabled

A "cripple"

Handicapped

Gimp

Marginalized…

I thought of nothing important on the drive home. The car seemed to park itself in the usual place.. I paced my rented house over and over, practically making new grooves in the wood. I paced and paced until my legs could no longer hold me, so I sat on my crème loveseat. I vowed to take up yoga, eat healthier, trade my dogs in for low-maintenance cats, live in a place without steps, or sneak into the radiology lab where my MRI results were stored and alter the report. Take out the words "multiple sclerosis." I rose, filled with this empowering thought of committing a crime.

I went into work early the next day to pounce on my busy boss before her day started. I was on familiar turf, now. In control. A rock star performer. I practiced saying 'multiple sclerosis' in front of a mirror at home until the words didn't result in tears

My boss, Katrice, passed my office and I yelled her name.

"Got a second, Katrice?" I said loudly, "It's important."

Katrice was the black body-type equivalent of me. We were both very overweight, but embraced it with high fashion and good grooming. She sat in my beige and wood armchair, and I heard her breath exhale sharply as she lifted the load off her legs.

"Katrice, I have multiple sclerosis. I found out yesterday. I don't know how this is going to impact my work... nobody does," I sound calm, and reassured her as she, not I, started to cry.

I shut the door to my office, returned to my black office chair, and recanted the whole history of my diagnosis.

My boss told me to take a couple weeks off. My doubles partner, a judge, owned a condo on Lake Michigan, so it was there I decided to retreat. I packed up all the girlie magazines I could find at Walgreens: Vanity Fair, Cosmo, Vogue, Family Circle, etc. I also took a case of beer, a carton of cigarettes, many packets of M & M's, and a journal. I decided that I would give MS two weeks of my time, and that would be it. I would return to work refreshed, healed, and the impact of MS on my life would be minimal.

Two weeks passed. I cried. I journaled. I participated in all sorts of vices. But I did not heal. In fact, now my right arm and hand were affected, too.

I went up and down the roller coaster that is MS. Over the years, as the disease changed its course, I adapted.

The next ten years brought out the warrior in me: MS took my vision three times, which I regained. I learned the world of quadriplegia four times when my hands, arms, legs, and feet all at once quit working. I bounced back, due to heaping doses of intravenous steroids. I lost my ability to walk seventeen times and had to learn to see the leg braces and canes as a warrior's fighting tools. I was the poster child for positive adjustment to MS and I spoke at conferences everywhere.

In my spare time, I was researching alternate careers that were less physically demanding. I took, and failed, the GRE but applied to several doctoral programs anyway. My first choice made me an offer: Michigan State University would give me a full-ride scholarship, if I came in to meet with the Director of the Rehabilitation Counselor Education program-- a program ranked number one in the nation, to explain my GRE's scores.

We met, and hit it off instantly. I was MSU's newest doctoral student!

Everything was happening fast: I sold my house in four days, during which time my mother passed away suddenly, and I was ensconced in student housing at MSU in two weeks.

Then, an MS exacerbation hit me with such force that I was no longer a big time warrior, fighting MS—I was a cripple who was stuck in an office chair in student housing. I could not walk. I could not sit up straight. I could not raise my arms. I hadn't gone out in public in two weeks, so I hadn't showered. The chair became my world as wrappers from sliced cheese created an ocean around me, and merged with the shame of being unable to use a bathroom. I hadn't made any friends in my program yet, and my neurologist was an hour away. I called his office, yelling with a voice that would stagger the Normal People, and said I needed help. This warrior had been taken down. I wiped my nose with the tee-shirt I had been wearing for two weeks: its advertisement was covered by the detritus from the gimp.

He said that I needed to be in the hospital and asked if I could get a ride to a facility in his city. But this was going to be more than a ride. I needed someone strong enough to carry me, too. Suddenly I remembered that I had a friend a half hour away who was a farmer. Strong and made of a laborer's muscle, Ginny could probably lift the foundation of the house I was trapped in easily.

I dialed Ginny's number. She answered after four rings and I verbally sprayed her with all the complications of my situation, practically in one breath.

Of course she would come over. Of course she would carry me to her truck. Of course she would drive an hour to the hospital. Of course she would pack my suitcase. That's what friends are for.

Of course.

I felt guilty as hell, and barely spoke as Ginny picked up the urine-soaked garbage that surrounded me. She wiped my face, and used the kitchen rag to clean my hands. I softly answered her when she asked me what I wanted in the suitcase. It didn't take long for her to pack me and my suitcase for the trip to the hospital that would soon connect the warrior back to the world.

The remaining, semi-experimental treatment for my worsening MS was chemotherapy with one of the agents used to treat people with leukemia. It would be rough on the heart, the doctors said. Plus, I was told by my team of knowing physicians that I may lose my hair if I gave it a go. I decided to take the chance.

After two weeks in the hospital, Ginny drove me home. I was using a walker to get around. I fell asleep propped in a chair and woke up to bright sunshine. I saw my lap virtually covered with licorice-like strands of hair whose highlights were still visible. I grabbed my walker and headed to the bathroom to shower. *Just Normal. Like Normal People do.*

"Well, fuck," I said as I extracted a quarter cup of soggy hair from my shower drain after completing my showering ritual. The pitted enamel that surrounded the drain looked like it survived decades of wear. *It's just hair. You can buy all different kinds of hair!* It was time to go shopping for some wigs to replace the rapidly dwindling supply of original hair on my head.

I was about to enter the "Cathedral of the Flowing Locks." I found the wig magazines, and ordered twenty wigs. The scripture on which the "Cathedral" based its liturgy was contained in a 76-page catalogue/hymnal filled with wigged models who sported do's that ranged from long and flowing, a la the Mother Mary herself—to short and sporty, like the Baby Jesus (if one was a believer).

I tried all colors and styles and would wear one to match my mood-of-the day. I could simply throw on hair and head out the door. I had hair for going to the grocery store. Hair for doing my daily walking. Hair for going to school. Conference hair. Hair that looked matted and askew for going to the bank.

I often evoked stares from passers-by... or was I just imagining it?

The majority of people glanced at my hips with disgust, as if they could see all the Denny's Breakfast Slams I had consumed in my lifetime. Was I hearing the silent: *"Poor thing's,"* Or, *"Good God. I better start 'juicing' in case I ever need to go on chemo and have to face people with a hairless head, like her."*?

It was the December Holiday Break in my doctoral program at Michigan State University. My hairs and I flew to Phoenix for a visit with my sister.

We were going to a New Years' Eve party of some of her wealthy friends. I prepped for the party in the dressiest clothes I had packed. Still, I felt out-styled by the other female attendees who donned 14k gold wrist cuffs the size of my neck.

I strolled among the boisterous crowd. I always kept a canapé at hand so I looked like I was busy doing something. I came upon a group of five women, including my sister, who were gathered like a flock of well-dressed chickens around a round table, buttressed by five-foot high heat lamps. I propped myself on the table, for balance. One drink stretched into four, and the hours passed in lively conversation about such news-making events like nail fills and heel height.

I began to smell something foul. It smelled like a car was burning oil. It was so noxious, conversation stopped as all looked for the root cause of the nasty odor.

"Jesus Christ, these rich people stink," I thought.

It was not me who first noticed the basis of the smell.

It was not me.... because it WAS me. My wig had caught fire from one of the heat lamps. Its strands were melting into one glob of polyester goo. I felt the heat on my head, and noticed how the five image-conscious women around the table were all pointing at me, speechless.

I began to bash myself on the head like a zoo chimp, and the hands of three others were flailing their arms in my direction, to get a shot at my head. My glasses went flying and a hand yanked down one of my Chico's necklaces in the fray.

"Oh my God! Dunk her head in some ice water!"

"Her head is probably burned! Let's go get some butter, or cream cheese!"

"Don't get too close! Your perfume will catch YOU on fire!"

I was getting pummeled by palm tree fronds, hands with heavy rings on them, the alcohol-tinged breath of the soused women, and veggie dip—thrown at my bangs.

So that's how I rang in the New Year of 2002. I returned from Arizona to Michigan feeling like a prize fighter warrior. I smiled as I thought of the flying spinach dip, and heartily laughed as I recalled all the horrified stares of the women who had been introduced to the life of a person with a disability, maybe for the first time.

A person with a disability.

Person.

Disability.

I am a person who happens to have a disability.

A person.

I drove from the airport back to my apartment. I was ready to resume my doctoral studies for a new term at Michigan State University. Most of the time I used the on-campus bus system, which had a stop near where I lived.

It was mid-January: a blustery winter day. A day where the snow swirled, and unbuttoned coats flew open. It was around 10 p.m. when I left school to catch the bus home. I stood in the dark with my cane along with other nearly frozen students at the bus stop. I wasn't waiting long when a huge gust of wind lifted my wig from my head and sent it rolling down the snow-covered sidewalk.

"My hair! My hair!" was all I could yell.

With great haste, three of my fellow travelers went chasing my hair down the long stretch of whitened concrete. The race was on. The hair appeared to be winning, as the figures grew smaller half a block away. The hair was still rolling, and the breath of the three pursuers formed a small cloud over their heads as they ran. Then, a pronouncement of success:

"Got it!" yelled one of my Samaritans. The three strangers headed back to the bus stop, one with a human hair-lined mitten. I thanked them profusely and inwardly laughed at what became an insane version of "The Tortoises and the Hair."

Nearly fifteen years later, at age 53, the disease is now attacking my brain and has caused a dementia that is secondary to MS. Like the movie 'Still Alice,' I am a professor who is slowly losing her memory to dementia.

But Julianne Moore can go home and remember her lines for tomorrow, whereas I cannot.

But warriors fight until the end. I refuse to be a 'cripple'. Defy the definition of a 'gimp'. And, I hate the word 'handicapped.'

I wrote another Haiku:

A KNOTTED ROPE LAYS
SPIRALED ON THE GROUND, THAT PULLS
HER TOWARD TOMORROW.

2nd Place

Sue Fagalde Lick

Oregon

Sue Fagalde Lick is a writer, musician and dog mom living on the Oregon Coast. "Tubes" is part of a memoir she is writing about living with her late husband through Alzheimer's Disease. She is the author of *Stories Grandma Never Told*, *Shoes Full of Sand* and *Childless by Marriage*.

Susan Fagalde Lick

Tubes

My husband always said he wanted no extra measures taken if he were dying. He even put it in writing. But I still wound up doing exactly what he did not want.

Shortly after Fred was diagnosed with Alzheimer's Disease in 2004, we met with our lawyer to draw up wills, powers of attorney, and advance directives for both of us. We checked boxes on forms saying we did not want to be kept alive with machines or feeding tubes if there was no hope of recovery. Our lawyer, Catholic like me, told us the church would want us to use a feeding tube. We still said no.

We never envisioned how things would turn out.

By 2010, Fred was living at a memory care facility called Timberwood Court in Albany, Oregon, 75 miles from our home on the coast. At 72, Fred was younger than most of the residents and one of the few who was physically healthy, able to roam the place without a wheelchair or walker. Staff recruited him to help with games, setting the table, and other simple tasks. Despite his increasing confusion, he remained calm, quiet and friendly.

But then things changed.

In early December, I started getting phone calls from Timberwood almost every day: Fred fell. He had a seizure. He wet his pants. He punched another resident. He pinned an aide up against the wall. They were giving him Ativan, a tranquilizer, to keep him calm, but the incidents kept happening.

One night, long after dark, I got another one of those calls. We had had heavy rain and thunder and lightning. My eye had not healed yet from cataract surgery a few days earlier. I didn't dare drive the treacherous highway east in the dark.

They put Fred on the phone. He was sobbing and couldn't form words. I promised I would come in the morning. One-eyed or not, I was driving by myself, not sure what I would face when I got there.

In the lobby, Rebecca, the activities director, told me she had spent hours the day before sitting with Fred trying to calm him down. He had been hitting people and angry. She got him to take a tranquilizer, but he started crying and wouldn't stop. He was still crying around 5:00 when she put him on the phone to me.

But now he was fine, all smiles and happy to see me.

We went out to the TV room, glad to have it to ourselves, but I couldn't make the TV work. It was almost Christmas. I started singing "Jingle Bells," and Fred joined me, singing bass. I moved from that into "Jingle Bell Rock." I sang all the lively Christmas songs I could think of. I didn't know all the words, but it didn't matter.

At last an aide came to activate the TV, and we settled in to watch an old episode of "Gunsmoke." But the music lingered in the air.

On the night we met, I was singing Christmas songs at a party. Music remained the shining thread that held us together in spite of Alzheimer's disease. When in doubt, we sang.

Now, Fred seemed clear of eye, clear of expression. He even had a sense of humor. When I said I had to go, he said, "No!" but he was smiling. We said a peaceful farewell at the door.

I drove out behind a truck with a sign that said GBF—Glory Bee Foods, glorybee.com. Amen.

The day of the Christmas party, Dec. 17, the nurse called me in the morning to tell me Fred had fallen. When I got there, he was sleeping by the TV and had a hard time waking up. I wondered if he had suffered a concussion or had another seizure.

He had a big bloody scrape on his forehead and another on the top of his head, both oozing through some kind of yellow ointment. Nobody, including Fred, knew what had happened. He was vaguely aware that he had an injury. He told one person he fell, another that he didn't.

Fred needed a shave and smelled like sweat. The aides said he had panicked when they tried to shower him. The water and soap would probably sting when they hit his wounds.

The Christmas party took less than an hour. Family members came. Santa and Mrs. Claus arrived, ringing bells, shouting "Oh ____, I've got a present for you." Santa posed for photos, asking, "Are you smiling? I am." Most of the residents had no clue what was going on, and I worried about how Fred was taking all this commotion. I kept thinking, "Get that f-ing Santa Claus out of here!" Santa passed out presents brought by family members and laden on a kitchen cart—his sleigh—then walked out shouting, "Ho, ho, ho!"

Why did they think these old people would get excited about Santa Claus?

In an hour, the party was over. Santa came, they passed out cookies and ice cream, and then the aides were cleaning up, asking, "Did you have a good Christmas?"

For Fred, the answer was no. My pictures from that day show a man who was battered, bent, and frightened.

At the party he was barely awake. He didn't understand that the sweatshirt I unwrapped for him was a Christmas present. It was noisy all around us as I quietly held his hand across the table in the crowded dining room until the party was over and we moved to the TV area.

That day was the first time I left Fred without saying goodbye. He was dozing in front of "Bonanza," twitching and clutching at his pants. I kissed his head and said, "See you later." He nodded as if he might have been aware. Then I punched the code on the door to the lobby and went out into the rain.

On New Year's Eve, I was waiting in line at a gas station on the way to Albany when my cell phone rang. The memory care center. They were sending Fred to the hospital by ambulance. He was suffering from severe abdominal pain, and they didn't know what it was.

When I arrived at Albany General, Fred was on a bed in the ER. The new sales director, whom I had not yet met, sat with him.

Imagine having a patient who cannot tell you anything, not where it hurts, when it started or what happened before. Guessing Fred might have appendicitis, the ER doctor sent him for an abdominal CT scan. It showed a super-enlarged prostate and a distended bladder.

While Fred screamed, "No! No! Please no!" three people held him down and a nurse shoved a catheter up his penis. The nurses said they had never seen so much urine come out of a person. The normal adult bladder stretches to hold a maximum of about 16 ounces before it gets expelled involuntarily—the person "wets his pants." But that hadn't happened. The enlarged prostate blocked the path between bladder and urethra so completely that Fred may not have urinated for days. Just thinking about it makes my own bladder hurt.

The plan was to keep him catheterized and send him back "home" with medicine that might shrink his prostate. But as the doctor was giving him one last check, Fred began to shake. He had a seizure right there in the ER.

The doctor ordered a head CT. It didn't show anything conclusive, but the doctor admitted him to the hospital. Fred remained unconscious in what's called a postictal state until the middle of the next day, when he woke up fighting the nurses and aides who tried to help him.

I spent the night in a motel room, celebrating New Year's Eve with a box of powdered donuts and Dick Clark's "Rockin' New Year's Eve" on TV.

Overnight, Fred had fallen off the cognitive cliff. Now he made up words and animal sounds instead of English, then looked at me as if I should understand. His hands trembled so badly he couldn't feed himself.

The doctor on duty didn't seem to hear me when I insisted he had not been this way two days earlier. She declined to order any tests or treatment for his seizures, citing his advanced Alzheimer's. She called in a physical therapist to walk him up and down the hall, then sent him back to Timberwood.

Fred could not urinate on his own. He tried, but nothing came out, so he had to keep wearing a catheter. He kept trying to pull it out and frequently succeeded. The female aides would gang up on him in his room to put it back in while he screamed and fought them with all of his 200 pounds. Suffering infections and frequently backed up with urine, he was sent back to the hospital almost every other day.

The staff started dressing him in what looked like a man-sized onesie, a flannel garment that zipped up the back so he couldn't get to his penis. Whatever dignity he had had before was gone.

More than half of men in their 70s suffer from enlarged prostates. Those without dementia notice the problem and see a doctor, who treats them with medication or surgery. Fred's problem turned into a crisis because no one suspected that he couldn't pee. He was still going to the bathroom on his own, but he couldn't find the words to tell anyone that nothing was coming out. By the time, he went to the hospital, his bladder was permanently damaged, and his dementia had advanced so far that nobody wanted to treat him.

Fred's primary care doctor suggested we just take out the catheter and let Fred die. His bladder would fill up and overflow, his kidneys would shut down, and he'd pass away in a few days. He would give him enough drugs that he wouldn't feel any pain.

Fred's bright pink POLST (Physician Orders for Life-Sustaining Treatment) form, filled out at the memory care center, specified that we did not want any extraordinary measures. No respirators, no CPR, no feeding tubes. The doctor was trying to obey it. But the form didn't say anything about urinary catheters, and Fred was standing right there, confused and frightened but very much alive.

Have you ever had a full bladder and been unable to go the bathroom for a couple of hours? Imagine how that would feel multiplied by days or weeks. I couldn't think of a more horrible way to go.

What other options did we have? A urologist down I-5 in Corvallis agreed to examine him. Determining that Fred would never be able to urinate on his own again, she suggested surgically installing a "supra-pubic catheter," a tube that would go from his lower abdomen directly into his bladder. Dr. O.

made it sound like a simple procedure. It would be permanent and less painful than the one in his penis. Supra-pubic catheters are often used for men who are paralyzed or who need permanent catheterization, she said.

Researching online, I read posts by men who loved their supra-pubic catheters because they gave them more comfort and freedom. It seemed like an easy solution to Fred's problem.

Fred was otherwise still physically healthy. If I let him die of a full bladder, instead of making him comfortable with the tube, wouldn't it be euthanasia? Wasn't I violating the rules of my Catholic faith? I consulted the Alzheimer's Association website, alz.org. They say that limiting treatments is not euthanasia, that it lets the disease take its natural course. I asked my priest. I wanted him to tell me what to do, to give me the definitive Catholic answer. He told me to search my heart.

My heart wanted an easy way out. Most of us in our Alzheimer's support group hoped that a heart attack, stroke, or something else would take our loved ones before the Alzheimer's got as bad as it was going to get. But this didn't seem to be it. This was just an enlarged prostate.

Meanwhile, the man I loved was a mess. He walked around in his onesies bent over, clutching at his penis. He battled with the aides and the nurse, and they kept sending him back to the hospital by ambulance.

On Jan. 21, the phone rang a little before 5 a.m. They were taking Fred to the hospital again. He had been agitated all night and kept trying to pull his catheter out.

Trembling from the shock of being awakened by the phone, I got up, showered, ate, dressed, checked road conditions, and packed an overnight bag while my yellow Lab Annie, awakened by my rustling, curled up on the couch.

I pictured the ambulance wailing down Southeast 14th, past Fred Meyer, past Albertson's, turning in at Timberwood Court, its red lights flashing in the dark parking lot as paramedics hurried in with their gurney. My mind went through all kinds of possibilities, partially fueled by too much time researching Fred's situation on the Internet. He might just have a catheter problem they could easily fix, but what if he needed emergency surgery right now? What if they refused to do it because of his dementia? What if he had an infection in his urethra, his bladder, or his kidneys? What if he was dying? Damn this long drive from here to there.

Was I about to become a widow in fact rather than in practice? Was it wrong of me to at least partially hope so? We had been fighting this disease for almost a decade. Nobody wants to live the way Fred was living now. But to die from unreleased urine? Please God, not that.

I hesitated to leave until it got light enough to see. At 7 a.m., I telephoned Timberwood for an update. Someone named Stacy said Fred was back from the hospital. They were getting him dressed and ready for breakfast.

"But what happened?" I pressed.

They reinserted his partially-pulled out catheter at the hospital and sent him home. Crisis averted. For now. So I wasn't going to Timberwood. I turned on the computer and tried to think about something besides Fred and his catheter.

I never relaxed anymore. Every time the phone rang, it was Timberwood.

In late January, another trip to the hospital forced a decision. After way too many phone calls and people talking at me, Dr. G. still wanted me to do nothing and let Fred die, but Dr. O. wanted to insert the supra-pubic catheter. There was a good chance it wouldn't work, she said, but she had already scheduled the surgery. Maybe he wouldn't pull this one out. It would be stitched in. He was never going to urinate normally again, and the doctors didn't see him as a candidate for prostate surgery, so this was our only option.

Was there a choice? I couldn't see one at the time. I was exhausted. My husband was out of his mind, and everybody kept wanting me to make decisions.

That afternoon, when I came back from a quick lunch break, Fred recognized that I was there. He said very clearly, "I'm in trouble."

Yeah, you are," I answered.

The next day, Dr. O. installed the supra-pubic catheter. Afterward, while Fred slept off the anesthetic, the hospital social worker made arrangements to move him to a nearby skilled nursing facility that accepted Medicaid patients. Timberwood was not equipped to handle post-surgical patients.

Fred was still unconscious when an orderly shoved him into an ambulance that took him to a small facility that looked like a rundown 1950s grammar school. They put him in a room with a man who screamed about how he didn't want a roommate. A nurse stripped off Fred's clothes and examined him for bruises, made me fill out a list of his possessions, and put him to bed.

All the while, the Super Bowl roared from televisions up and down the hall. It got late, and I had to work the next day. Fred was still unconscious. I left for the coast, knowing my husband would wake up in an unfamiliar place where he didn't know anyone and would not understand what had happened to him.

It was two weeks before I saw him awake again. The staff told me he did get up and try to eat, but whenever I arrived he was always in bed, muttering, twitching, his hands shaking. His new catheter, which looked like a TV cable sticking out of the area between his belly and his penis, was mashed against him by a thick bloodstained elastic bandage.

Eventually he woke up, but he was a zombie. Stoned on tranquilizers, his dementia much worse, he didn't make eye contact. He sat for hours fingering an inch of curtain or the bottom of his shirt. He didn't eat. He didn't talk. He didn't walk. Staff moved him between bed and wheelchair like a sack of potatoes, ignoring his moans. They diapered him and cleaned him like a baby.

When he was up, Fred's catheter bag was wrapped around the frame of his wheelchair. He kept trying to get out of the chair and occasionally succeeded, falling on the floor. Dr. O. had said to wrap the bag around his leg, but they didn't do it.

On a Thursday night, the supra-pubic catheter stitched into Fred's bladder got pulled out. Either he pulled it out with his hands or it got yanked out when he tried to escape his wheelchair. No one reported it until Monday. By then, the hole had begun to close up. Fred's bladder was full again. The nurse on duty that night was fired, and I was invited to file a complaint, but what good would it have done? Dr. O., notified on Monday morning, was livid. She reinstalled the Foley catheter into Fred's red and raw penis and scheduled surgery to redo the supra-pubic.

On March 13, after I had spent hours in the surgical waiting room, a nurse came to tell me that that day's first attempt to insert the tube had failed. It was too close to the enlarged prostate and wouldn't drain. Dr. O. did the operation again a couple inches over. The hospital sent him back to the nursing home with two catheters, the one in his belly and the other coming out of his penis. Soon both tubes and the bags below were lined with blood clots and puss. Another infection.

Fred didn't eat, talk or respond to anything. He had lost 30 pounds since Christmas. Always a burly man, he looked bony now, bony and old. I sat beside his bed and his wheelchair for hours, singing to him, holding his hand, trying to reach him. His hair was long, his beard overgrown. His hands would crawl toward his catheter. I would move them away.

Sometimes when people talked loudly in the hall, he would respond. Once he yelled, "What?"

"It's okay," I said.

Now I think about how I comfort my dog when she's having a bad dream. "It's okay," I whisper," petting her gently. She sighs and relaxes. It seems like the same thing.

I kept hoping for a flash of recognition from Fred. Nothing.

When I went to leave, I kissed him on the lips. He made kissing motions with his lips, perhaps an automatic response. At least he seemed peaceful, which gave me hope. Maybe in some way he knew that I was there.

April 19 was a gorgeous day, the fields deep green, the sky blue with puffy clouds, the air smelling of mowed grass.

At the nursing home, Fred seemed more animated. I had asked that his dosage of Seroquel, a strong antipsychotic drug, be reduced. He looked around, seeming to actually see things, and he talked quite a bit, although his words were almost impossible to understand. He didn't reject my hand this time. He smiled at me now and then, almost laughed once; he tried to sing along with the music on the radio.

He probably felt better with no catheter in his penis and no diaper, nothing under his pants. I worried about not having the backup catheter, but at least now there were signs of Fred actually being in there. When he smiled, I felt a weight lift off of me.

We made noises and winked at each other. When it was time to go, I kissed him, hugged him and told him I loved him. As I started to walk away, I heard him say something. I turned back. "What?"

"Yes," he said.

Thank you, God.

That was the last word he ever said to me.

On April 22, while I was singing with the church choir at a Good Friday service, my cell phone rang. I wouldn't usually answer it during Mass, but the call was from the nursing home. The night nurse told me Fred had fallen that day and "taken a turn." She thought he might be dying. Did I want him to go to the hospital, she asked? No. On this, the POLST form was clear. If he was dying, he would die in his own bed.

At 2:30, he had another seizure. Around 5 a.m., he vomited blood, and then he died. "Expired" was the word the nurse used.

His death certificate cites several causes of death: upper GI bleed, advanced dementia, enlarged prostate with urinary retention, hypothyroidism, and seizure disorder.

Too late for Fred to feel the relief, his tube was removed. The staff cleaned him up, but he still had blood in his hair and his beard, and his expression spoke of torture.

My guilt is immense. How different is installing a tube that removes waste from putting in a feeding tube? When Fred first became ill, he asked me to use Oregon's assisted suicide law to help him die. I told him I couldn't do that. Not only am I Catholic, but the Oregon law requires that the patient be close to death and fully aware of what he's doing. That can never happen with Alzheimer's.

In hindsight, I should have let him go. Yes, the staff at Timberwood could have gotten him care sooner. Maybe with earlier treatment, his prostate would never have become a big problem. Yes, the nurse who didn't report that Fred's suprapubic catheter had been pulled out deserved to be fired—and she was. Yes, I could have sued, and I might ultimately have gotten some money, but that wouldn't have helped Fred. I had different doctors telling me different things, and I thought I was saving my husband from a horrible death.

The prostate is one of many body parts. If a man with dementia had appendicitis, would you let it kill him? If he had a broken arm, you'd get it set, but what if he needed surgery to make it right? What if the problem had been in his heart? Would we have done open heart surgery? What if he just needed a pacemaker? He already had a fatal illness. How do you decide? Where do you draw the line? What is too much?

Alzheimer's patients are considered poor surgical candidates. The anesthesia worsens their dementia, they don't understand post-op instructions, and they unwittingly do things like pull out their tubes and IVs.

If the checked boxes on Oregon's POLST form specify "no extraordinary measures," the doctors can't do anything to revive a patient who is actively dying. If he stops breathing, they cannot resuscitate him. But the form doesn't say anything about not being able to urinate.

On Fred's advanced directive, he initialed the statement saying he didn't want his life to be prolonged by life support or tube feeding. If suffering from "an advanced progressive illness," it says, "I want my doctors to allow me to die naturally."

I knew there would be no respirators, CPR or feeding tubes. But the catheters fell into a gray area where nothing legal was being violated. Supra-pubic catheters are more common than most people know, but their complications bear a frightening similarity to those associated with feeding tubes. An Alzheimer's Association brochure on end-of-life decisions notes that use of a feeding tube can result in infections and the need for physical restraints because the person may try to pull out the tube. Fred experienced both of these situations with his catheters. He suffered constant infections and spent too much of his last few months being held down or sedated while people forced tubes into his body.

In weighing the pros and cons, the brochure asks: "Will the treatment create physical or emotional burdens?" If you're a man lying naked on a table naked with female doctors and nurses shoving tubes up your penis and into the area a few inches above it while you're screaming "No!" is this not a physical and emotional burden?

The person most affected could not tell me what he wanted or how he felt. And what kind of choice did he have? Would you like to die in agony in a few days or over the next few months? I thought I was doing the right thing, but now, four years after his death, I think I know what he would have said. I stand in front of his urn at the cemetery and beg his forgiveness.

What would you do?

3rd Place

Yvonne Kariba

District of Columbia

Yvonne Kariba loves writing as much as she loves inspiring and motivating others to be better versions of themselves; she started her blog www.schoolcalledlife. wordpress.com in an effort to do just that. She is the author of the upcoming book *Make Things Happen; Traits & Habits of Successful People & How You Can Develop Them.* Yvonne believes that we are all students of life and have something valuable to teach and most importantly, learn from each other. She is a contributing blogger to the Huffington Post blog, addicted2success, the everyday power blog and the change blog. Her aspirations are to become a best-selling author and speaker someday. Yvonne is the mother to a brilliant and very energetic son who is just as curious about life and enjoys keeping her on her toes. You can connect with Yvonne on twitter @ykariba or LinkedIn.

Yvonne Kariba

Defining My Beauty

Being a woman in today's world is extremely challenging. Every day, we get bombarded with images that tell us what we need to look like and have allowed society to dictate the definition of beauty. Women are, unfortunately, unfairly and harshly judged based on their appearance and because of this experience pressures men don't have to endure and would never be able to comprehend.

Unrealistic standards of beauty promoted by impeccably photo-shopped and digitally enhanced images of beautiful women that stare back at us from glossy magazine covers contribute to a majority of women feeling dissatisfied with their looks when they compare themselves to said images and feel like they don't measure up to what is purported to be the ideal.

This has resulted in us women becoming our own worst critics when it comes to judging ourselves and pointing out our flaws. We strive for perfection that doesn't exist and chase after an elusive ideal that serves only to make us feel more insecure about ourselves in the end and leads to the poor body image issues we sometimes struggle with.

Nearly fifteen years ago, I decided to bite the bullet and made the courageous decision to shave off all my hair. I didn't do it to be rebellious or make a fashion statement of some sort, but more so because I was genuinely tired of allowing my hair to control me and having society tell me what I had to look like to be considered a feminine woman.

I had beautiful medium length permed hair before making this decision that was at times untamable and as a result had me crying like a baby whenever it wouldn't cooperate. I am embarrassed to recall the number of events I failed to attend because my hair didn't look right or wouldn't behave when I tried to style it, thus contributing to a sour mood.

I loathed spending endless hours at the salon on Saturday afternoons waiting for the hair dresser to attend to my hair instead of at the mall shopping with friends or just enjoying a lazy day in the comfort of my home. I also hated forking out my hard-earned money on a myriad of hair products that over-promised a mane as beautiful and silky as a horse's and under-delivered as far as said guarantee was concerned. To say that my hair ruled me would be an understatement; it owned me!

I can still remember the look of dismay on my hair dresser's face the day I made the "fateful" decision to shave off my hair. I had woken up one fine Saturday morning with the fixed decision that was the day I would finally put an end to all the madness I had allowed my hair to put me through. I called her to set up an appointment and made my way to her salon with the simple mission in mind; Operation: Get my life back!

You would have thought I had told her I was planning on joining a Covenant in Timbuktu when I told her to cut off all my hair. "What do you mean, cut off all your hair?" she asked in a shocked voice. "Just exactly that", I calmly replied, "Shave it all off!" She spent the next half hour trying to talk me out of it with the threat that I would regret the decision and said that she wouldn't support me in my decision. She finally relented when she realized just how serious I was and that I would take my business elsewhere if she carried on being stubborn, didn't she know that the customer is always right?

I felt liberated and lighter both literally and figuratively with each clump of hair that fell to the floor as she passed a pair of clippers through my head. I was relived to find out that I had a decently shaped head under all that hair and was very pleased at the image that stared back at me in the mirror. I couldn't believe how beautiful I looked, my new hairdo really showcased my facial features and made them pop, if I may say so myself; maybe this wouldn't be so bad after all.

I remember walking out of the salon taller and with boldness I didn't know I possessed that afternoon. I loved how confident my new do made me feel and knew I had made the right decision in shaving my hair. Heads turned as I made my way down the street imaging I was strutting down a catwalk instead as I swayed my hips from right to left and held my head up high. A few people stopped me to compliment me on my look, while others asked if was a model; I guess that was the kind of aura I projected that day.

A lot of people were very receptive of the change while others struggled with understanding why I as a woman would want to have a bald head; wasn't a woman's hair her crowning glory? Wasn't Rogaine formulated because people were trying desperately to combat baldness? They doubted I could truly feel beautiful without hair and tried to convince me to grow it out once it came back in.

My Mother wasn't the least bit thrilled about my new hairdo and immediately went into defense mode when she next saw me, telling me that men preferred women with long hair; to prove her point; she even took things to an extreme and conducted a little survey asking men if they would date a woman with short hair. It didn't matter to me what they all said or thought, I was happy with my decision and determined to never grow my hair or allow anyone to influence or dictate my appearance choices.

I noticed that I attracted a different caliber of men upon shaving my hair. The men that now seemed drawn to me were conscious minded, highly educated and referred to me as "Queen". I thought it was very interesting that they all confessed they loved my natural look, were attracted to me because of my hairdo and wished they could convince the women in their lives to follow suit. It amazed me that there existed a great number of men who still considered me very feminine despite my lack of hair; I guess like Shakira sang, my hips didn't lie and helped convince them that I was the real deal and still very much womanly.

What stood out the most though was that a majority of the people that loved my new look kept commending me for being so gutsy and courageous for having made such a bold change. They seemed to imply that I had balls for defying society and choosing to dance to the beat of my own drum instead. Women confessed that they wished they could define their own beauty and not care so much about what others thought of them, while the men applauded me for embracing my own individually and refusing to become a cookie cutter image of what society seemed to be shoving down women's throats as being men's preference and ideal.

It amazed me that what I personally considered to be a small change garnered so much attention and inspired many stimulating conversations that affirmed my thoughts; society really does play a huge role in dictating and influencing our views on beauty. As flattered as I was that people thought I was courageous for choosing not to conform to its standards of beauty, it saddened me that a great number of people didn't feel comfortable enough being themselves and defining their own meaning of beauty; they felt they had to accept what they had come to believe to be the ideal.

I loved not having to wonder about what to do with my hair every morning and that I could wash it each evening when I took a shower. It was wonderful not having to worry about my hair getting ruined whenever it rained and I hadn't carried an umbrella with me. These might seem like trivial matters to most but to me, they meant a great deal. I loved that my hair no longer controlled my decisions or reigned over me. I could now dance in the damn rain if I so well pleased.

If you know a thing or two about black women, it's that we are very fixated about and into our hair. We don't like getting our hair wet if it has a relaxer or weave in it, don't allow our men to touch it or run their fingers through it lest their fingers get caught in our weave tracks, and above all, we really don't mind spending astronomical amounts of money on our hair's upkeep; some women have been known to sport weaves more expensive than the average home's down payment. Black women's hair requires a great deal of maintenance because of its coarse and sometimes overly thick texture, fortunately, relaxers, weaves and braids assist in making its maintenance easier for many of us.

I was glad that I no longer had to deal with the pressures my hair once imposed on me. I felt free and in control and loved that my new do was not only manageable but very easy and cheap to maintain. I soon learned how to shave it myself and acquired a pair of electric clippers. I must admit though that shaving my own hair made me feel a little masculine at times, having someone else do it made me feel pampered and taken care of. I soon got over that when I realized how much time and money I saved by doing it myself.

My hairdo seemed to pique curiosity among many; it always amused me whenever little girls approached me to inquire whether I was a boy or girl. It seemed my lack of hair confused and puzzled them as they had most likely grown up brushing their Barbie doll's hair and wishing for similar long tresses themselves. As young and innocent as they were, they too attributed long hair to femininity and beauty and made the naïve assumption that any woman that sported a bald head was either a man or cancer patient. The also all seemed to agree on the fact that they would never shave their hair if asked to, unless they were donating it to someone who needed it more than themselves.

I encountered some ignorant people as well upon shaving my hair that made quite some interesting assumptions about me based on my hairstyle choice. A couple of people assumed I was and even accused me of being a lesbian because of my bald head. Those that weren't quite sure had the audacity to inquire if that was indeed the case as though my sexual preference was any of their business.

I couldn't get over their ignorant stereotype; the fact that I didn't have any hair somehow implied that I wasn't feminine, probably had some masculine tendencies and was most likely attracted to other women and played the male role in the relationship. I really didn't know whether to laugh or get annoyed at this assumption. I love and embrace all people and don't believe anyone should be made to badly about who they are, I happen to also be very secure in myself; although their assumptions didn't offend or bother me, I couldn't help by feel appalled by our tendency as human beings to rudely judge and label others based on their appearance especially if it differs from ours and our personal preferences.

My mom continued to get on my case regarding my hair despite noticing how happy and confident my new do made me. She suggested that I try growing out my hair on several occasions and even remarked how much prettier I would look if I put a texturizer on it and got a pixie hair cut; she just wouldn't let up on this issue. Although I knew that she meant well with her suggestions and concerns, I couldn't help but feel disappointed that she didn't approve of my new look; I couldn't understand what the big deal was.

I once got into a minor tiff with a complete stranger at the Metro Station regarding my hairdo as we awaited our train. A man who didn't know me from Catherine or Jane remarked on my hair and venomously stated that women like myself who wanted to be like men were the reason so many problems existed in today's relationships, and that he would never date a woman that didn't have hair.

I wondered what his problem was and why he felt he had the right to criticize my hairstyle choice seeing that it didn't have any direct impact on his life and he didn't know me personally. I reminded him that it was MY hair and I could therefore do with it as I pleased and also assured him that the feelings were mutual as far as not dating each other was concerned since he really wasn't my type as I prefer intelligent men who exercise discretion over shallows ones as himself. I guess he considered himself very fortunate when our train pulled into the station shortly.

I had a hard time comprehending why some people were so opposed to my haircut as though it had something to do with them or was a reflection on them in some way. A lot has changed since then; natural hair is now widely celebrated and embraced. A lot of women have discovered the dangers of the chemicals they use to "relax" their hair and just how toxic and damaging to the hair they really are. I recall burning my scalp on several occasions when I used to perm my hair and how much the chemicals had made my once thick hair thin. It seems they are counter-productive and more problematic than their worth.

After some time, I did something I vowed not to do that made me feel like a major sellout and a little disappointed in myself; I allowed my mom to convince me to grow out my hair. I really don't know what made me throw in the towel, I think I was just quite frankly grew weary of her suggestions and decided to just humor her knowing I could always revert back to my do if and whenever I chose to.

As excited as I was at the prospect of a makeover of some sort once my hair came in, I couldn't help but feel like I was starting to let my hair control me again, I worried about what to do with it once it grew to a considerable length, my options were to either loc it to texturize it which didn't seem too appealing to me. I missed my bald head and the lightness I once felt and how free my head was. I now wrapped my head in beautiful headscarves a majority of the time or donned fashion forward hats that sometimes resulted in headaches as my head wasn't used to being so constricted.

The more time progressed, the more I realized just how unhappy I was; I didn't like the fact that I had once again allowed people's expectations of me to dictate my actions and decisions. I woke up one morning and decided enough was enough; I was through with being untrue to myself and would finally respect the small voice within me that had been telling me for some time that I needed to get over everyone's expectations of me and embrace my individuality.

I stood in front of my bathroom mirror and passed a pair of clippers through my thick head of hair. I felt a sense of liberation greater than that I had experienced when I first shaved off my hair. I guess the reason for this was because this time around my decision was made despite knowing very well that it would ruffle a few feathers based on my past experience and would most likely be viewed as a "screw you" kind of move.

I wasn't going to let any fears or society's expectations of me place me in a box; I would dictate my own rules and make decisions moving forward that allowed me to express and embrace my authentic self. I realized the reason a majority of people that loved my hairdo thought I was courageous for making such a move was because my action had represented fearlessness to them.

It has been said that courage isn't the absence of fear but the conquest of it. I realized that I had overcome fear when I let go of my need to please everyone and when I stopped worrying about what others would think or say about me because of my lack of hair. I had finally overcome the need to look like all the women that stared back at me from the glossy magazine covers because I finally realized that I was and am perfect just the way I am.

Yvonne Kariba

4th Place

Cheryl Romo

California

Journalist Cheryl Romo is an award-winning investigative reporter and essayist. She is the former editor of Common Cause, Sacramento, and The Fortnightly magazines. Much of her recent work has been focused on disadvantaged children with mental health needs. Romo is a graduate of the University of San Francisco and was a Casey Fellow at the University of Maryland.

Cheryl Romo

Golden

December 2006

Every day for four days, the doorbell rings and the postman comes. The cardboard boxes arrive, one-by-one, just before Christmas. I can't open them. Not yet, not now, perhaps never. I carry the boxes upstairs to the spare bedroom, stack them together, and shove them under a long, gray table in a spare room. I cover the boxes with a forest-green curtain and leave them to ferment.

The patient husband downstairs doesn't ask why his eccentric wife is making a shrine under a table nor does he ask why teacups must be arranged in threes or why rock piles are placed between plants all over the backyard of the house they have lived in for a dozen years. The one they moved to just before... The patient husband keeps drinking his black coffee and eating peanut butter toast and reading the *Los Angeles Times*. He pretends life is normal. "Do you need any help?" he says.

No one can help me. Don't you see I'm making a shrine?

Over the years, the spare bedroom has become a museum of memories. It is painted golden yellow and has a large picture window that overlooks a peninsula with homes dotting up the summit of what locals call "the hill." This mountain, which rises from rocky cliffs carved by the Pacific Ocean, was once considered sacred by the indigenous people whose footsteps disappeared long ago. But the blinds in the golden room remain closed. For a mother who has lost her child violently, there is no sacred.

49

My son's name was Steven. I feel him everywhere, especially when summer comes with its crashing waves and red suns. Then I imagine him sitting on a white beach with his red surfboard beside him. I smell his suntan oil. Before the cardboard boxes arrived, my son's widow called. A last request, she said. "He wanted you to have his books. He wanted you to tell his story. If you can't, he asked that his library be donated to The Abbey of New Clairvaux in Northern California."

Good God. Where did this come from? I didn't know my son was a Catholic. The Steven I knew was a free thinker, a rebel who said he didn't believe in organized religion. Yes, I've made my living as a storyteller. As a journalist, I write about the lives of *other* people. Did I fail my son? Is this a penance?

For seven years after my son died, I consoled myself by writing stories for a newspaper about children who died in foster care. Many of these innocents had died at the hands of caretakers who were supposed to protect them. When I tried to uncover the facts surrounding their deaths, I became a pariah among the adults who hid behind a veil of bureaucratic secrecy. What did I care? My son was gone. I wore "pariah" as a badge of honor. But the time came when I had done what I could do, when others were willing to step forward to continue the fight, when it was time to step back and reflect on what my life had become. I left my job.

In the aftermath, my grief returned ten-fold. Writing was no longer my solace. The only place I felt alive was in the garden. There, thoughts of Steven overwhelmed me. Even ten years later, it was a pain that wouldn't go away. But I digress. My gut aches, my head splits and my neck stiffens. *If Steven had finally come home, where was he?*

Outside in the garden, I stand in the chill and mist of winter to prune last roses. The thorns rip skin on my fingers and they bleed. Fortunately I find enough late blossoms to provide an awkward bouquet to welcome my son home. Because other family members, who are unaware that I have an invisible guest in my spare bedroom, will soon arrive for the holidays, I decorate the Christmas tree with ornaments passed through generations of sentimentalists. I go through the motions and brush my hair and wash my face and put on a smile for the patient husband downstairs.

While cleaning my home office, I open a file drawer and lift out an old manila folder marked "Steven." A piece of pink paper drops out. I recognize the handwriting but don't remember receiving the message. The undated note reads:

Dear Mom,

I just wanted to tell you how much I love and think about you. You are truly a beautiful woman and a light in my life. Your friendship has meant the world to me. It is great to have a mother such as you.
I love you,
Steve

Dear God. There's a happy face drawn at the bottom. But a decade of grief has wreaked havoc and I find that I'm no longer able to comprehend declarations of love. Ten years since the midnight phone call telling me that Steven put on his best clothes and prayed before he chose to greet death. How could I *not* have known? Why couldn't I rescue him? You see, I once knew a happy child who liked wearing costumes – cowboy, soldier, businessman, sailor, baseball player – and this boy had a father and a mother and a little sister who loved him. We were a good family before Steven's father lost himself and disappeared from our lives. When Steven was eleven, his father committed suicide. People say children are resilient, that they bounce back from trauma. But those people don't see the scars beneath beautiful faces and sweet smiles. Suicide isn't a simple bounce.

After my first husband died, Steven didn't react. He did all the normal stuff children do: Little League, swimming, skateboarding, bicycling, sailing. Back then, we rented a tiny cottage at the beach and we went camping in our yellow Honda every summer. We had dogs and cats and Steven was perpetually finding injured birds and nursing them back to health. I remember the time he found a seagull with a broken wing and insisted I take the bird to the pet hospital. When the vet told him the gull wouldn't survive, Steven held the bird in his arms as it was euthanized. The gull's memorial service afterward included flowers and prayers. All the children in the neighborhood came.

Early on, Steven demonstrated a talent for writing and music. He wrote poetry and played guitar. During the birth of punk rock, he was the first on the block to have one ear pierced and to let his platinum hair grow to his shoulders. I'll never forget the night I found him in the bathroom painting (ala Kiss) his face white and trying to pencil a black star over his eye. When not emulating his favorite musicians, Steven read everything he could get his hands on by Stephen King, Edgar Allen Poe and Mark Twain. But his favorite book was Kahlil Gibran's *The Prophet.*

During his teenage years, Steven began experimenting with alcohol and drugs. He explained his behavior by telling me that he was trying "to function like normal person." It was not normal and I was worried. Family counseling helped, as did visits to a male psychiatrist who believed the self-destructive aspects of my son's personality represented an "adolescent identity crisis." But there were deeper problems and, as a single parent struggling to support myself and two children as a newspaper reporter, I was completely over my head.

Still, even in trying times, Steven made me proud. Unlike his peers, he never swore. Instead, he called people funny names like "celery head" and "radish breath." He looked after his little sister and adored his grandparents. "I'm a dancing fool," he used to say. But he wasn't a fool. He was smart, funny, popular and sensitive.

Surfing, a sport he'd fallen in love with as soon as he was tall enough to lift a board, provided a healthy outlet. I loved that he always smelled like suntan oil and ocean salt and that everything about him was clean and fresh. In the late seventies, the boys who hung out at our house began talking about joining the U. S. Marine Corps. They thought all Marines were macho men and beyond cool. After high school, the dancing fool was the only one to sign up.

On the day of Steven's graduation from boot camp at Camp Pendleton, I had never seen him so proud of himself. Not long after, he was sent to Japan and letters and photographs from Okinawa began arriving in my mailbox. He seemed happy, *really* happy. Then something happened. I don't know what it was and he never talked about it. But the stress of regimentation or what Steven called "arbitrary rules" shattered him. A Navy psychologist in Okinawa recommended my son for discharge. But his superiors in the Marine Corps had other ideas. They saw him as a screw-up. One night his roommate came home and found Steven cutting his leg with a scuba knife. Steven was hospitalized. After his release from the hospital, the military brass continued to see him as a "disciplinary problem."

That's when I received another letter from Okinawa. Steven wrote that he wasn't coming home. "In my eyes, life is not worth living and I don't want to go on suffering," he wrote. Thanks to services provided to families of service members by the Red Cross, I was able to intervene and Steven was shipped back to Southern California where he could receive counseling. But he was still a Marine and he spent another year stationed at Camp Pendleton in San Diego until his discharge.

The first thing he told me after leaving the military was that he was joining his father. "It's my destiny, Mom."

My heart broke and it was the day I grew claws I didn't know I had. "No, it isn't," I said.

It took time. Self-help groups eventually turned Steven's life around. He began to believe in himself and talked about becoming a non-denominational preacher. The years tumbled by as I held my breath with crossed fingers and watched my son mature and settle down. He began attending college and he was reading and writing again. For a time, he moved in with his elderly great-grandmother and helped her in ways that were unbelievable. They became a charming odd couple before my son fell in love and married Marcy. The wedding, he said, was the happiest day of his life.

The last time I saw him alive was New Year's Eve 1995 at his sister's wedding in Sacramento. Before the ceremony began, I was approached by a stranger from the shadows. When the man touched my shoulder, something shot through me like a bolt of electricity. The hurt in the emerald-green eyes was palpable. "You don't know who I am, do you?"

My voice cracked. "I'm sorry," I said. "Sweetheart, you look different. You look like . . . ." I stopped, not wanting to say what I saw. Steven was pale and thin. He'd dyed his blond hair black and it was slicked back into a modified pompadour, a style popular when I was dating his father in high school. My son had affected a clipped British accent, wore black-framed glasses, and looked like the imitation of a ghost.

"I look like Dad, don't I?"

After the wedding, we huddled in a corner and talked into the morning while I tried to figure out what was going on. A transformation was underway and I didn't know how to stop it. In hindsight, how could a mother be so stupid as to *not* recognize her child? *What was wrong with me? What was wrong with him?*

A couple of weeks after my daughter's wedding, I came home from work and discovered a phone message. "Mom, I'm leaving," Steven said. "Moving to Idaho." When I called him back, no one answered. In my mind, "Idaho" will always be a synonym for death.

On Valentine's Day 1996, I was home when the phone rang.

"I belong to God now," he said. "You are no longer my mother."

After he hung up on me, I couldn't breathe.

May 1996

One night, I had a vivid dream. *There was a fire in my house. No one was home. When I arrived, three firemen covered in soot were waiting on the lawn. They explained that the house had been saved. But the electric organ, the heart of the home, was gone.*

The next day was May 15. It was close to midnight when the phone rang. My daughter-in-law spoke in a flat voice. "Steve's dead," she said. "He shot himself after I went to work."

Like a robot, I sat sobbing in the shadows at LAX waiting for the first morning plane bound for Sacramento. By the time I arrived in Redding several hours later, two sheriff's cars were parked outside and a uniformed officer was putting a hand gun into a brown paper bag. "You're the mother?" No words needed. "The body's already been moved."

I entered the small, white-frame house and went through a narrow hallway to a bedroom that doubled as an office. Other than a bullet hole in a wall and towels covering what I assumed to be a bloodstain on the green-shag carpeting, everything seemed orderly. Tidy even. I closed the door and opened drawers in the desk. I examined every scrap of paper. I meticulously went through Steven's brown-leather wallet: no money, credit cards, just a driver's license and a Red Cross blood donor card. His gold wedding band was sitting on the desk, next to spare change that didn't add up to a dollar. A bible with a *Name of the Rose* bookmark was opened to *Psalms* on the desk. A highlighted passage told of being sinful from conception. .

Steven was thirty three.

His father had been thirty one.

We only *bought* two years?

Before I left, Marcy handed me an envelope. "He wrote this for you on Mother's Day," she said. "I thought it was beautiful. He was always writing you and never mailed any of it."

The gift my son had left was a card with the picture of a golden angel on the front. Inside, Steven said he loved me and was "disgusted with how the demons of life have divided us so." I didn't know what he was talking about. The message continued in a rambling, chaotic fashion and he said someone was trying to kill him. "When I reflect back on my life I see what a wonderful mother you truly were to me," he wrote. "I love you and am sorry for having hurt you. When all of this is over I want to be your friend again."

That night, I checked into a nearby Holiday Inn and tried to sleep. But the room smelled of Hexol, the disinfectant I used in baby Steven's diaper pail. A voice in my head kept repeating the phrase, "Take care of the living." I recognized his voice.

The next morning, the coroner released the body to a funeral home. Gulping coffee from a Styrofoam cup, I drove a rental car to a run-down, red-brick mortuary on the wrong side of town and was allowed to see my son, swaddled in a royal-blue blanket on a gurney, in the annex next to the mortuary's chapel. I could not lift the blanket. Steven looked emaciated – and I stroked his hair, black gone, gold again, until a strong wind burst the chapel door open. I took it as a sign that it was time for me to leave. When I walked into the mortuary hallway, I was cornered by the pie-faced funeral director who reeked of cigarettes.

"You're the mother, right?" I nodded. "Well, that boy in there shot himself through the heart. It was suicide. *Suicide*," he said, spitting the word out. "I don't know how you're going to live with that."

I didn't know either.

A month later, a memorial service was held at our home. Everything went wrong. The electricity, inexplicably, cut itself off; food that was supposed to be delivered went, instead, to the porch of a vacant house down the street; wine-soaked mourners hurled insults, mostly in my direction. In hindsight, it could have been worse. Had there been more candles, we could have seen each other.

April 2007

For a decade, I had greeted Steven in shadows and dreams. It took months to find the courage to open the cardboard boxes. When I did, I found that the archives of Steven Kirk Romo consisted of four well-worn bibles, one hundred twenty two books, dozens of pamphlets on various Catholic saints, three photo albums, two book bags stuffed with writing, a picture of Jesus, a miniature replica of a black Porsche 911, and a pouch full of religious medallions. There were no books by Stephen King, Mark Twain or Kahlil Gibran. However, there were complete collections by John Wesley, Thomas Merton and dozens of other writers I'd never heard of, most with the abbreviation for "saint" before their names. It was clear that my son was a man desperately in search of God.

Each morning, I sat barefoot in a purple bathrobe and pulled out books – first two, then three, some old and crumbling – from the boxes. In the beginning, I planned only to make a list of titles and authors to send as an accompaniment to books I planned to mail to the monks at the Abbey of New Clairvaux. Reading religious books was not on my agenda. But, as I opened each volume to find copyright dates and publishers, Steven's messages – written inside cover pages and throughout the text – hooked me.

Many of the volumes were hand-decorated or painted and featured photographs of my son's favorite saints, writers, family members and musicians. Here and there, I discovered photocopies of pictures of Steven as a toddler and a teenager. Soon I was fanatically transcribing the deepest thoughts of a wandering soul – and forgot that dinners must be cooked for patient husbands and the dog walked and life lived in the present. Instead, I burned sandalwood incense and scented candles and popped burritos into the microwave. When I did go to the supermarket, I bought flowers and neglected to buy food. I was inside the greatest mystery of my life.

Nearly every book was signed in a familiar handwriting by someone I didn't recognize. "When your luck is bad you can either change your name or your life," he wrote. "I shall change both." My son had become Steven K. Anthony, the black angel, a desert monk who belonged to a new knighthood called the De Novae Militia. The name Anthony had been borrowed from St. Anthony the Great, leader of the so-called desert monks in the early days of Christianity. It took me awhile to figure out where the black angel part came in. The black angel had been discussed in the *Book of Enoch*, one of the Gnostic gospels, a book included in Steven's library.

"What is a black angel but one who has become an outcast from his fellow human beings," my boy wrote. "The black angel, like the phoenix, rises from the dust and ashes of the fiery flames of hell. The black angel lives. God brought him back from the dead."

Why did my son think himself an outcast?

"I am a monk, a monk without a monastery, a desert monk," he explained. "There is only one true friend and he is God. Seek him above for you are alone. . . .I wish, above all things, for death to fall upon me. My greatest of all fears is to live a long and powerless life left at the hands of sadistic human beings with no deliverance, except from the master of the house of death. I feel the reaper today eagerly awaiting my arrival."

Notes written in a book called *Preparation for Death* by St. Alphonsus De Liguroi indicated Steven, who described himself as a damaged vessel attempting to navigate through turbulent seas, made careful preparations. "I have a feeling this will be the last book I ever read," he wrote. "My time to die is near. Dream big and dare to fail."

Though I knew the ending, each time he wrote that he was a "new man beginning a new day," I cheered. And his sense of sick humor was intact: "Property of Steven K. Anthony, the black angel, the desert monk, philosopher, metaphysician, logician, religious apologist, mystical theologian, prophet, sage, behavioral scientist, super sleek, super sexy, super cute, supersonic, hip, slick and sick. The higher type, the Teutonic blond beast, the ultimate warrior, the ultimate man and, by providence, to soon become the greatest writer of the 20th century, the anchorite, the lonely one."

It took months to transcribe my son's words and hours to pack the boxes again. Had Steven died of natural causes or in an accident, would I have felt differently? In the final months of his life, Steven was in anguish. At the back of one book, I'd found a one-way baggage claim check to Honolulu, the place where his father died. He'd printed his dad's name on the claim check. The children of suicides are eight times more likely to commit suicide.

In November, I drove five hundred miles to the Abbey of New Clairvaux, which is located in the rolling green hills and farm country in Vina northeast of Sacramento. The monastery is bicycle close to where Steven had lived with his wife. I arrived the day after Thanksgiving on a quiet afternoon. Brown leaves fluttered down from the branches of century-old walnut trees and fall foliage created a soft-brown carpet on the ground. I stood at a concrete half-gate and pressed a bell. Moments later, two men riding in a golf cart approached.

"You rang the bell?" asked the driver, wearing a red flannel shirt, blue jeans and work boots.

"Yes, I did. I'm looking for Abbot Thomas. I have an appointment."

In September, I'd written the abbot to tell him about Steven's request to donate his books. Abbot Thomas said the monks would be delighted to receive books for their library. But he asked me to wait until November. November is the month when the Catholic clergy traditionally prays for the souls of the dead. I knew this because each year since Steven died I've asked the Jesuits at the University of San Francisco, where I attended school, to pray for him.

"This is Thomas," the driver said, pointing to his passenger, a slight man wearing a black Dickey sweatshirt over black-and white monk's robes.

The seventy-four-year-old abbot stepped out of the golf cart. "I didn't know your son," he said. "But I'm sure there are monks here who remember him."

"He loved this place so much," I said. "My son's books are in the back of my car. I think we can fit the boxes in the storage bin of the golf cart."

But the monk in the flannel shirt was already tooling up the road. "Whoops," Thomas said. "I missed my ride."

We drove my car to the abbey offices and left the boxes outside on a stone ledge of the building. When I looked back, the boxes formed the shape of a coffin – and I could feel pressure rising in my chest. For the next hour, we walked along tree-lined paths and Thomas X. Davis told me about his home. Clairvaux means "clear valley" or "valley of light." The abbey is a Cistercian-Trappist monastery, a place of silence, solitude and separation from the world's distractions. "I've been here since the beginning," Thomas said.

The abbey was established in 1955 on land once owned by Leland Stanford, a former California governor. It is a working farm and the monks raise money by selling prunes, English walnuts and grapes. As the afternoon sunlight filtered through the trees, we walked up and down the roads, some little more than leaf-strewn lanes. The abbey, which is self-sustaining, is a simple sanctuary with tangled English bramble gardens. Until recently, the monks took vows of silence and poverty. It seemed impolite to ask why they continued to embrace poverty but decided to begin speaking. Thomas' job is to function as "the representative of Christ" on the grounds. "The purpose of the order is to teach stability and patience," he said. "Everyone must work."

He directed me to turn around and pointed to a one-story building. "Your son would have stayed there. These are the contemplation rooms for our guests." Each of the rooms has a sign of virtue on the door. Room number one is love. In addition to the contemplation rooms, there are two rustic guest cottages, a small library, a bookstore and a dining center. The family of one of the monks, a man who looked to be about Steven's age, was visiting from Hawaii. Children were laughing and playing ball on the lawn while women cooked in the kitchen. Thomas said abbey buildings where the monks live are off-limits to visitors. "But your son was probably allowed to use the library where we have 30,000 books," he said.

On this day, there was chanting inside St. Cecilia's Chapel. Thomas said the monks were rehearsing for Sunday services. The four men standing inside a pew singing made an ethereal sound that bounced off the ceiling and walls. In the chapel courtyard, I was immediately drawn to an unusual statue of the Virgin Mary. She was handing away her infant son. "This statue was created because of a dream," Thomas said, explaining that the woman who had the dream asked the monks to find a sculptor to recreate the image she'd seen. "I wasn't sure about it at first," he said. "But I've come to like it."

As we were about to say goodbye, Thomas mentioned that Thomas Merton, one of Steven's heroes, had been his teacher at the Abbey of Our Lady of Gethsemani in Kentucky. I didn't know why he mentioned it because I'd told him nothing about Steven's books. "That's it, then," I said, stumbling over my words. "There are dozens of, uh, of . . . Thomas Merton books in my son's library." Our eyes locked. Thomas asked me to come back. I didn't think I could.

In New Clairvaux, Steven believed he had found sanctuary. He wrote that the monks accepted him, gave him reading lists and encouraged him to worship in the chapel. But the only thing I felt driving away was that my son had finally gone home. After returning to the peninsula, I asked my husband to come upstairs to the golden room. It was time to open the blinds. As we walked in, I noticed something on the floor and picked it up. It was a snapshot of Steven and his great-grandfather. In the photograph, Grandpa Bill, who lived to be 96, was holding a baseball and an adolescent Steven was wearing a baseball cap. Both of them were grinning.

I dream of an afternoon when an orange-red sun shines bright over silky water and a boy with emerald eyes and golden hair stands at the batter's mound with a Louisville Slugger. I watch the bat connect and the ball go flying like a comet into the powder-blue sky. I see the boy glide from base to base. When he comes around the curve, I watch him slide across home. The crowd roars. Our eyes connect.

Cheryl Romo

4th Place

Barbara Ruth
California

Barbara Ruth is a photographer, poet, essayist and fiction writer as well as memoirist. Sadly, she has been unable to ride a bike for over 40 years, due to disability. Her work appears in the following 2015 anthologies: Lunessence: A Devotional For Selene; *QDA: Queer Disability Anthology; Stories Of Our Lives: Women and Health; and Slim Volume: This Body I Live Inside.* She is a daughter of Yemaya; Ashkenazi Jewish, Potowatomee, and Welsh; a member of the neuroqueer community; a yogi; a film festival enthusiast; an animist whose spirituality is informed by Native American, Sufi, Buddhist and Jewish Renewal teaching;, a vegetarian for 40 years; an eco-anarcha-feminist; a housing justice activist in Silicon Valley, and an out lesbian everywhere she goes.

(photo credit: Barbara Ruth)

Barbara Ruth

Out Of Luck

In 1955, the summer I turned nine, I increased my distance every day. My parents had given me an odometer for Christmas, silver, like the trim on my blue Schwinn, so I knew exactly how much. When I could ride ten miles in one direction I started packing a lunch and announcing to my parents, after breakfast, "I'm going on a bike hike."

"Be home in time for dinner," Mom would say and off I'd go into the long humid days of southern Michigan, from our house on Canaris Street west to Highway 131 where it traveled north with St. Joseph River, or south to White Pigeon, nearly in Indiana.

By late July I'd made it up to 30 miles round trip. *Good for a nine year old kid*, I told myself. I never said, *Good for a nine year old girl*. What was there about endurance bicycling a boy could do better than I?

Sometimes I left my glasses at home, for the myopic thrill. I was never afraid of getting lost, worn out, unable to pedal home, although Mom insisted I take dines for the pay phone, just in case. I loved finding new country roads beyond the limits of the village of Constantine, beyond pay phones, loved feeling my sweat evaporate as I pushed against the waiting air, into wherever the road would lead me.

I turned right on Youngs Prairie Road that day. Maybe I'd stop at Mary Ann's for lunch.

Mary Ann was a farm kid, part of my gang, the girls who had slumber parties every weekend. Not my best friend, that was Laura, but someone with whom I shared the mysteries of childhood.

I lurched over something - a shard of glass, a sharpened stick, a snarl in the road - and there went my front tire.

My bike was unrideable. This had never happened before; I had no plan. I started pushing and pulling my bike along the road, fingers wrapped around the handlebars.

When the black truck pulled to a stop beside me I smiled in at the man driving it. He looked a little like Elvis, only older and not as handsome, with his acne and scruffy moustache. Here was a better way to get my bike to Mary Ann's, where one Dad or another could drive me home. There were a few houses on Youngs Prairie Road but I didn't know who lived in them. The only idea I'd come up with was to get to Mary Ann's.

"Looks like you need some help," he said.

"Boy, do I! I have a friend who lives less than two miles from here. If you could give me a ride, maybe her Dad could fix my tire."

"Sure. Get in. Throw your bike in the back of the pickup."

I squinted through the open window at the gap toothed smile. My bike only had a flat, it wasn't totaled. "Could you help me lift it in? I don't want to throw my bike around."

He shrugged. "I don't feel like getting out of the car. You can put it up here in the cab, behind the seat, if you think there's room."

Adults were always doing or not doing unexplainable things. It did seem better, having my bike up where I could keep an eye on it. I'd had a flair of worry when he said to throw it in the back: would he drive off with it? This way my bike would be right where I could turn around and see it.

He reached over, pulled the lever and folded the passenger seat forward. His arm was over it now, reaching out toward me. The black hair on the light brown skin looked like the arms of lots of the Dads I knew, creepy but normal. I lifted my bike, straining under its weight but determined to get it into the back seat. He took hold of the handlebars and I pushed the back wheel and together we wrestled it into the back. "Okay," he said, "You next."

I listed my left knee to get my foot onto the floorboard, grabbed hold of the door handle, and hoisted myself in. I smelled whiskey, just like when I rode with Dad. And then I saw his thing was out, in his left hand. I looked anywhere but there.

"How do you like my truck?" he asked.

"I dunno. Nice, I guess."

"Nice! It's a beaut. It's a '48." That made it two years younger than me. Why would anyone be proud of a truck that old? "It's in cherry condition."

Teenage boys said that about cars, I knew from the older brothers of my friends. They said it about girls, too, and then it sounded dirty, just like the way he said it now.

"I can see you take really good care of it," I tried. I'd been with enough drunks to know better than to tick one off if I could help it.

"You oughtta take better care of that bike," he said. "You should have watched where you were going."

"Maybe so." My mind was racing, trying to figure out what to do, what to say, and at the same time wanting to just go blank.

"Lucky for you I came along. Lucky for you I let you put your bike in my truck."

Hadn't I thanked him already? "It's nice of you to give me a ride to my friend's house. Thank you very much."

"What's your name, anyway?"

"Mary Ann," I lied.

"Well, Mary Ann, I think I'm going to charge you for this ride. I want a kiss."

Once when I was five and my dog wasn't there to protect me, the big boys cornered me in the woods and told me I had to give them a nickel or pull down my underpants, I remembered, as I considered the dimes I had in my pocket. "How about I give you fifty cents," I said. "That's all I have."

"That's not nearly enough for all this trouble. Your filthy bike is messing up the back of my cab."

He hadn't started the car. The backs of my thighs stung from the horsehair digging through the cracked plastic seat cover as I made a list of what I needed to do: open the door, jump out, pull the seat forward, grab my bike, haul it out of the truck and get away. But I just sat there, frozen in the sweltering truck.

He grabbed my hair and pulled back my head, then his face was on top of mine. His moustache scratched under my nose. His tongue went into my mouth and I thought I would choke. His fingers pinched me everywhere and the wheels and handlebars of my bike poked into my shoulder and somehow I was on the gear shift and he was on top of me, pushing the air all out of me, and how had he gotten under my shorts and shirt and oh! it hurt so bad where I peed and what was this gunk on my leg?

He breathed hard for a while but mostly he remained very calm, a calm I recognized. It likely meant he wasn't mad, so he probably wouldn't kill me. This was all sort of familiar, but whatever it almost reminded me of, I didn't want to think about. I tried to straighten up my clothes instead. Finally he said, "You go on now."

"I need my bike." My voice was small, girlish, not my voice at all.

He pushed me out and I fell hard, half on the asphalt, half on the dirt. My bike landed on top of me, torqued a way it shouldn't, the back wheel spinning and spinning.

"See ya," he said, and drove away.

I have no idea how long it took me to drag my bike the mile and a half to Mary Ann's house. I stopped a few times where the trees could hide me because I kept having to pee. Elm leaves crinkled in my hands as I gathered them, rubbing my thighs where the gunk oozed down, trying to wipe it away. No cars passed me on Youngs Prairie Road, and when I turned onto Brick Chapel Road, where Mary Ann's farm was, I'd mostly stopped crying and bleeding. I glanced up the few times I heard a car, made sure it wasn't the black truck, the cherry, then lowered my head, let my hair hang over my face.

Mary Ann was in the tire swing in front of her house, kicking her bare feet where the grass had been trampled down. Her auburn hair was sliding out of her pigtails and the top button of her red and black madras shirt was open. My right hand flew to my own shirt, feeling for buttons I didn't remember checking after it happened. I couldn't find the one in the middle, the one that lately strained a little to stay closed. My shirt had been open since back there on Youngs Prairie. On top of everything else.

"Hi." Mary Ann stopped scuffling her feet as she tilted her head. "What happened to you?"

"Are your parents home?" I asked. "What about your brothers and sisters?"

She frowned, stood up out of the tire swing. "Mom took them all to Three Rivers. Dad's out fixing the tractor in the barn. What's going on?"

We went inside. Soon into the telling we both decided I needed to take a bath. "You told him your name was Mary Ann?" she said, faintly, when I came to that part. "Why did you do that?"

"I don't know! It just came out. What difference does it make?"

"It just makes me feel like it happened to me, too. I wish you'd made up some other name."

Maybe I had been trying to pretend it happened to a girl who didn't have my name. But I should have made up some name like Gretel, from an old story, a name nobody had nowadays. "I told you, he got me on Youngs Prairie Road. I never told him I was turning on Brick Chapel. Maybe he's from Indiana, or some other state. There's no way he can find you."

She was quiet for awhile. "I'm sorry he got you."

"Do you think your Dad can take me home?"

"Yeah. He'll have to take you in the truck, and your car can go in the back." I thought I would throw up when she said that but it still seemed better than calling my parents. At least Mr. Wilson's truck was red. "We'll tell him you fell off your bike and you can't ride it home. It's better that it's him. My Mom would ask questions."

We found band-aids for where I'd scraped my hands and knees when he pushed me out of the truck. I put toilet paper inside my underpants.

My parents were both home, playing honeymoon bridge in the kitchen, the fan blowing directly on them. "Is that you, Barb?" Dad said as I came in the front door. "Short ride."

"I fell," I called out, before they had a chance to see me. "A dog jumped out in front of me and I swerved to miss it and I fell. Lucky I was on Brick Chapel Road. I just walked my bike to Mary Ann's. I took a bath there because I got scuffed up on the pavement. My bike's pretty busted up. Mr. Wilson was working on the tractor today and Mrs. Wilson wasn't home. Mr. Wilson said he didn't have time to try to fix my bike, so he just brought me home."

I was into the kitchen by the time I finished this speech Mary Ann and I had rehearsed. "Oh, honey," Mom said. "You are all banged up. I'm glad you could get to Mary Ann's. Your knees must hurt."

"You got bandaged up I see," Dad said. "Any other damage?"

"The bike."

"We'll get it fixed," he reassured me. "I'll have John Thomson come over with his tools tomorrow and we'll work on it."

"That's just like you," Mom said. "Swerving so you wouldn't hurt the poor dog. And then you and your bike took a tumble. You have the worst luck."

She said that about me a lot. "I guess I do."

That afternoon I walked over to Laura's house. We went up to her bedroom and turned on the radio like we always did when we shared secrets. We sat on Laura's bed and I told her and we held on to each other as we cried and cried. "Do I still smell funny?" I asked. "I think I do."

"You just smell like sweat. the kind of sweat when you're scared. Don't worry about that part. What if you get pregnant?" Laura stood, and ran a hand through her curly black hair as she frowned. She took out hankies from the top drawer of her dresser and brought us each one. They both had L embroidered in the corner. "Could that happen?"

"I don't know. I bled down there but it stopped. Do you think that makes a difference? But weren't we scared last summer that we could get pregnant from boys peeing in the pool?"

"Yeah, but then the older girls said that wasn't true. Anyway, I think you're too young," she said doubtfully, although our whispered sex education included stories of girls our age who had gotten pregnant in countries no one we knew had ever been to.

Laura asked me again and again what the man and the truck looked like. I was already sort of forgetting. "How tall was he?'

"He never got out of the car. What does it matter?"

"Because he said, 'see ya.' If we spot him from far away, driving or walking, we need to run." I was grateful she said 'we.'

Laura and I did look for him, for months, long after we'd decided if I was pregnant I'd somehow know by now. Every time we saw a black truck that might be the cherry one my guts clenched like fists and I'd put my head down or turn around and Laura stopped breathing. "It's gone," she'd finally say. "We're safe." I think I did see that truck a few times, in the next two years I lived in Constantine. I always ran down a side street or into a store and my belly cramped up like I had stomach flu.

Neither Mary Ann nor Laura ever suggested I tell. I knew with absolute certainty if my parents found out I would be blamed and that would be the end of my bike hikes. The worse fear I had about getting pregnant at nine was that everyone would know what I had done and I'd never be free again.

I did ride my repaired bike, not as far or free as before, and never on Youngs Prairie or Brick Chapel Road. I decided I hated cherries.

I was ten when I first heard the word rape. My friends and I were trying to puzzle out why it always said "rape" in the newspapers and "fuck" on the abandoned buildings. What was the difference, anyway? I learned from Chrissy, the lawyer's daughter, there was statutory rape and regular rape. From my Black friend Jeannette, I heard about the Scottsboro boys, who were accused of rape by white girls who just said it because of prejudice. Someone had a cousin who knew a girl who went to the police because a guy raped her. The cop said if she took it to court it would be like she was raped again.

I was glad all of this had nothing to do with me.

In 1977, returning with my friends to Philly from the Michigan Womyn's Music Festival, we stopped at my parents' house in a different small town in Michigan. After three days of camping we were grateful for real showers and beds and sofas to sleep on. We were all drinking pink lemonade when my mother started telling me about the rapes near the bridge over the Grand River, where the cliffs are. "Four young girls," Mom said. "I guess it's dangerous there now. I hope they catch him." She showed me the latest newspaper article. My immediate reaction: How did the first girl have the guts to tell?

"The way these girls dress, with bare midriffs and short shorts, I'm not surprised it happened." The ice cubes clinked in Dad's martini glass.

I looked up from the article. The feelings of vindication: *I was right not to tell* and humiliation: *I'm so ashamed for my friends to see what my father is really like,* flooded me simultaneously. "It says here one of them was just twelve," I said.

"Girls who are twelve don't look like twelve these days," Dad said, exhaling the sigh that always followed his first swallow.

"Rape is the fault of the rapist." My voice quavered. "Not the clothes, not the location, not the victim. Rape is the fault of the man who rapes."

My father looked at me, then my mother. "When's dinner?" I couldn't eat the huge fresh salad, every ingredient from Mom's garden, she'd fixed especially for me.

In 1994 my parents visited me in West Marin, California. They tossed lines back and forth about my happy childhood, pitching and catching relentlessly, as though they'd rehearsed, all the stories that began, "Remember the time?" and proved how normal we were. "Everything was fine," Mom said again, "until you went to college and got in with a bad crowd."

There were so many things I could have almost said. "I was raped when I was nine!" I spat it out into the shocked silence. "And I was right not to tell. .Because of what Dad said about those girls who were raped in Grand Ledge."

"What girls?" he said. "I don't remember."

"I do," Mom said, and then she turned to me. "But there's things you don't know, either." Her face had turned pale under her short white hair and her eyes were like English walnuts, glistening in the rain of her tears. "About that same time, when you were nine, Dad and I had planned to go away for the weekend. You were already babysitting your brother by then but we thought you two needed an adult in the house for overnight. I had a hairdresser whose husband did a lot of babysitting. They really needed the money and she begged me to give him the chance to stay with you kids for the weekend. I thought I should be fair - not discriminate because he was a man - these days I'd say I didn't want to be sexist, I guess - but I just had a bad feeling so I told her no. That man was arrested for molesting the children he'd been babysitting." The tears were on her cheeks and in her voice. "I tried to protect you."

I swallowed hard as I felt my chin tremble with my own sobs, rising up. "You did, Mom. You trusted your intuition and protected me from that babysitter. Thank you."

They went back to their hotel and I thanked my lucky stars they weren't staying with me. I sat on my deck, letting the rustle and scent of Douglas pines and the bright trills of two flautists playing Bach down the canyon replace the sour echoes of our words.

The next day my parents, who'd been at least cordial, and in some cases loving to my lesbian friends and lovers over the years, announced they now understood what "made me a lesbian." I said the obligatory words: that I celebrated my lesbianism, and no man had had any part in its creation. And I asked myself: what had I gained by telling them about the rape? I'd done it - picked the horrible thing for which they were the least culpable - to put an end to their insistence about my happy childhood. I wasn't ready for more confrontations from my litany, a list I'd been making as I gradually filled in the blanks in my mind. And I sure didn't anticipate giving them a reason to pathologize my lesbianism.

I did lose something that summer day in 1954. I lost my casual daring, my no glasses, ride as hard and long as I could embrace of the world. I became more fearful, more wary of men and trucks, more prepared for breakdowns and falls. I have vowed to never let my fear stop me, and when it does I make that vow again.

I'd like to say I told all the girls in Constantine about the guy in the black truck. I hope at least I told my friends besides Mary Ann and Laura: Chrissy, Lois, Jeanette, Sue, Carole, Pat, Delilah, Charlene. Did he get one of them? Did anyone ever stop him? How would I know?

Only now, 60 years later as I write this, do I ask: "If I had told, if I had somehow found the right words, the right time, the right person, could I have stopped him? Could I have saved some of us? It isn't my fault, there's no way to know, I was only nine years old, for God's sake. Did I choose my tattered freedom over the safety of my beloved girls? Is this lump in my heart survivor's' guilt? The spokes spin and spin, spin and spin. I am still searching for leaves from the trees by the side of the road, trying to wipe myself clean.

Honorable Mention - Alphabetic Order
Judy Light Ayyildiz
Virginia

Judy Light Ayyildiz conducts writing and women's seminars. Internationally published, she has been a litmag editor, a writers' conference founder, and a musician. 11 books in 5 genres sprang from her life and teaching. A cross-cultural triumph-over-trauma memoir, ***Nothing but Time***, was 2002 Virginia College Bookstores' Award Finalist. Poetry, **Mud River**, was acclaimed by Fred Chappell and William Packard. Novel, **F*orty Thorns,*** was released in both Turkish and English. She is also author of a children's book, and four co-written supplementary writing and critical thinking textbooks. 4th volume of poetry in 2015: ***Intervals —Appalachia to Istanbul.***

We Gather Together

Within the month that I began teaching at Lucy Addison High School, my mother called to tell us that she was coming across the mountains to live with us in Roanoke, Virginia. She adored my boys, and she sure as heck couldn't figure out why a woman with two young'uns would want to teach when she had a man who was willing to pay the bills. Most important, our three-year-old had touched a grandmother's heart, luring her with: "Ganny, I don' wan' go gool. You keep me?" That was all she needed. Furthermore, she let me know that she was a bit concerned with my having taken the position of being the only full-time white person on staff at Roanoke's African-American high school,

A year previously, I had joined a women's group founded in 1908: The Thursday Morning Music Club. As a young professional musician, I figured to associate with a group that had helped in founding the Roanoke Symphony Orchestra. I sang in the club chorus and enjoyed the other performances of special programs.

That year of 1968, I'd been appointed as the TMMC's Hymn-of-the-Month chairman. My job was to present to our sizeable group the history of the hymns, chosen by the national organization. Our dignified lady members assembled at twenty round tables that were all dressed out in stemmed glasses, flowers, silver, and dogwood china in the Hotel Roanoke's elegant Crystal Ball Room. My role at the meeting was described in the by-laws. After reading the history, I was to introduce my choice of a musician or musicians, who would sing or play the hymn. Following that, we'd eat lunch. Desert ended with a distinctive musical recital selected by the local board. Being free to choose the artists that I wished enabled me to highlight new talent. The selection for November was the well-known "Thanksgiving Hymn." By the last of September, I had devised a special treat for the illumination of that song. It involved the appearance of my Lucy Addison students.

When I told my Addison choir that we were going to sing for the Thursday Morning Music Club, they thought it was far out and way too cool baby, as they had never sung for a white audience on white territory, and especially in a space like the Crystal Ball Room—where most of them knew somebody who was a tuxedoed waiter on the hotel's exquisite all-black staff.

At first, my Addison singers kept prodding me. Was I dead <u>sure</u> that we could perform there? The famous hotel, originally erected by the railway to accommodate its elite passengers, sat prominently against the skyline of the town, but decidedly on what was commonly known as, "the colored side of the tracks." Most of my students had never even been on the hotel's grounds. Their nervous questioning sounded as if what they were really saying was, "Are you positive that it's even <u>legal?</u>" I reassured them, and handed out copies of the hymn, arranged by me so as to particularly show off their voices. I was so proud of these kids; felt certain the club ladies would not only be surprised but delighted with them.

I ate my lunch every day with the shop teacher, an older man who had taught at Addison for years. His kind eyes and humorous way had me feeling right at home. If I didn't understand something that I needed to know, he was the mentor who set me straight. One day, I told him that I thought I had a problem, and I wasn't sure how I should handle it.

"The kids have started to call me, 'Mamma,'" I whispered. "It's too personal a way for a teacher to be addressed. What should I do?"

"No kiddin? They really be calling you, 'Mamma?'" He leaned across the table and said in a loud voice, "Hey, Miz Judy's students now calling her 'Mamma!" I was embarrassed. Now, everybody in the lunchroom would know. I was surprised that my confidant would expose me like that.

The others reacted as if it was an award or compliment, saying, "All right, Miz Judy!" My mentor looked back into my face.

"'Mamma' is the highest title of respect they could give you." My mouth fell open. "They calling you 'Mamma' already? Hot damn! Lady, you're _in_ with them. What do you do? You don't do nothing. You just be glad with it."

In the next few weeks, we began to perfect the hymn, with me drilling the various sections in phrasing, line, and tone so that each sounded like one voice that blended and balanced with the rest. My Addison Choir did not sing a hymn with the plodding reservation like most groups I had heretofore known. They felt the rhythm of each measure and phrase—eased themselves effortlessly into the joy of the poetry so that the gratitude embedded into the stanzas became what the hymn was all about.

The school shipped our rather worn blue and white choir robes to the dry cleaners. I envisioned my choir's mood of festive celebration flooding across the pink tablecloths and flowers of the ballroom.

The choir informed me that their former director, the retired and revered Mr. Gray—who, unexpectedly and unfortunately had left Addison last spring because he had gone blind—held an extra rehearsal one night of every week of the school year. They were used to coming out for that, and it had become a social work time. Mr. Gray also owned a popcorn machine and served them snacks and drinks afterwards. How could a skinny girl like me compete with a devoted and beloved teacher like that? I couldn't. I had to be me. It was natural that they just didn't know how to take me at first, but they were polite; and were warming up to me—to "Mamma." Telling them that I had no popcorn machine but they were welcome to bring snacks and drinks, I added that would meet them at the school at seven o'clock on Thursday evening.

Mother had a fit. "You can't go driving alone over into that section of town at this time of night! You have children to think of."

"Exactly, Mother. My singers will all be there." I hated to frustrate my mother but I felt a duty to my students. And the idea rather reminded me of church choir practice.

When I drove into the parking lot, a group of young men huddled in a cluster on the edge of the dark concrete block. I latched my door, and then swerved so as to shine my lights onto them. Hands came out of pockets and they waved to me. Waiting, were eight of my tenors and basses.

One of them took a sashay over. He bowed and opened my door. Another came up to remind me to lock my car. The basses and tenors intermingled and hummed around me until we were inside the building. After rehearsal, they walked me back out to my car, and stood there until I turned at the bottom of the hill toward the thoroughfare. I was more than well chaperoned.

Our rehearsals were going great. After we fine-tuned the hymn for twenty minutes, we'd start in on the Christmas program. The choir's sitting in the chairs was for learning and drilling at certain points. Getting sent to sing on the risers meant they were ready for polish.

The week before the hotel performance, the acetylene-clean robes hung in their clear plastic bags. We practiced walking up onto the risers like pros, with our music cupped at our sides. We rehearsed opening the weatherworn music folders in unison. I wanted a perfect effect on the ladies. Some of my students would have family and friends working at the hotel. I wished that the whole African-American community could hear them sing, "We gather together" in the Crystal Ball Room.

At that last Thursday night's rehearsal, I arranged with the janitor to have the risers taken to the hotel early on the morning of the event; and then, went home rather tired. Performance was one week away.

At home, the next evening after dinner, the phone rang. It was the music club's program chairman. Cheery to reply who was going to perform, I told her, "The Lucy Addison High School Choir." There was a pause. Thinking the line had gotten disconnected; I glanced from the shiny dial face to the wall plug.

She cleared her throat. "I'm sorry, I didn't understand you. Would you give me that name again?"

When I slowly repeated it, adding that it was my school choir and that I had written a special arrangement of the hymn for the occasion, there was another silence. "Hello, are you there?" Finally, she spoke again.

"How many of them are there?"

"Sixty-two. Oh, don't worry, we have our own risers, and they will be delivered and picked up from the hotel without any disturbance to the club."

"Sixty-two?"

I hesitated. "Yes."

"I don't think that would be allowed."

"I don't understand. It's my job to select the hymns' performers."

"But sixty-two, uh, Negroes? The members wouldn't know what to do."

Getting riled, I said, "They would sit back and listen to them sing, "We gather together to ask the Lord's blessing...."

"Please," she interrupted, "I know the song. I'm sorry, I'll have to get back to you."

When she hung up, I went to pacing the room, fuming. Mother came in. I ranted, "...and they are a Christian club, and what does she expect those children are going to do to the ladies in that ball room?"

"Honey," Mother said, "You've overlooked the obvious fact that you're living smack dab in the very state that was none other than the capital of the Confederacy." And then, just to get in a plug for the home state, she added, "Where'd ye think ye were, in West Virginia?"

"That was long ago, things have changed! The Civil Rights Act passed in sixty-four!"

"That may very well be, but you can't be going crossing boundaries like that on your own. You should have asked me before you got involved in doing something reckless and half-cocked like that." The phone rang again.

It was the president. She told me that she had just had a telephone conference with the club's executive board and it was decided that the members would be too uncomfortable with sixty-two teen-agers running around in their midst. However, if I wanted, I would be permitted to bring one soloist from the choir. "One can nicely represent the whole choir," she added in a southern honey lilt.

This was too much. I advised her that they would not be running around anywhere. "They are rehearsed to file into the room in measured order, onto the risers," I quipped.

"Out of the question. Did you not understand me?"

My throat thickened so that it was difficult to speak; but I pushed on: "My beautiful young singers, who still hold out the hopes that enlightened people can be good and fair humans beings, will sing the hymn..."

"You're making this more difficult than it need be."

I sniffed and coughed, aware that Mother's hand held across her mouth. "...and then they will file out and get on the bus and return to school...."

"I'm very sorry, Judy. Moments like this are what make my job hard."

On that, I took a breath and gained energy and passion. "I'm absolutely aghast that my choice of presentation of the hymn as stated in the bylaws is not accepted. You, dear lady, are the one that's making the job hard."

"I am sure that is the way you see it. But, your rudeness is not necessary. I have to inform you that the club, when they asked this job of you, had no idea that you would go to such extremes on an issue that has never before been opened."

After hearing from her once more that I did not seem to comprehend that this predicament was settled in the called board meeting. I could choose only one student. My tears flushed as hot as my red was face. With trembling voice, I stated, "You should be ashamed to deliver such a demand to me. There is nothing, nothing about this decision that's just. I will not insult my choir by bringing one member!"

"As I said," she repeated, "I'm sorry."

I retorted: "You and your lousy bunch of bigoted, you, you can find a performer more suited to your type for the

"Thanksgiving Hymn;" and furthermore, I hope you choke on your turkey while hearing the words of the song. Tell your executive board that I immediately resign from this prejudiced club!"

"I hope, young lady," she said with a wizened leer, "that you will live to see the error of your ways."

From the stress of emotion, I could hardly move my mouth; so I talked through clinched teeth. "Remember this: The world is changing. Discrimination is evil. There will come a day when you will not only have black singers in your midst but you will have black members sitting at the table with you, and you will be happy to get them, for otherwise, you will not have a club." I was on a roll. I took a breath and geared up in a quieter and firmer voice. "Yes, I am a young woman, and you are, unfortunately, not. That's true. Perhaps only one of us will live to see that day."

"The club happily accepts your resignation," she said coldly.

"Good," I answered, and laid the heavy black receiver into its cradle. Mother took her hand from her face and stood shaking her head slowly. The board must have already discussed my possible resignation. I got my jacket and went out into the back yard to deal with the emotion under a cold moon that looked like it had tilted onto its back. Little could I know that my prophesy of the club would indeed come about before the turn of the century

I connived with my mind all weekend as to how I could tell the choir. By Sunday afternoon, I had to admit that I dreaded having to deal with the situation at all. It was like being forced at the last minute to tell your groom that you weren't going to marry him after all. I had fleeting thoughts of how to avoid facing my students—call in sick, leave town for an extended stay, or just quit my position. Even though Mother said, "Just tell them the truth and be done with it," I lacked the resolve.

Rather, I rehearsed with myself of dancing around the upcoming event as some sort of bothersome obligation that I had second thoughts about doing. After all, we had our big Christmas production. The kids might suspect that something was amiss; but perhaps they would just let it go. In my heart, I did not believe any of that, either.

Mid-morning on Monday, the choir straggled in through the door to the music room by twos and threes, to stand around exchanging headlines of what they had done over the weekend. I leaned over my desk marking off the attendance chart and nodding back as they called greetings to me. I let them socialize for a couple of minutes following the blatant class bell. Like armfuls of catbirds in a huge box, students' voices danced on the high green walls. My ears filled with the reports of birthday party outrages, news of a boyfriend's making a fool of his own self again, and a taffeta pink dress with no shoes to be found to match in all the stores in town.

Lost in staring at the binding on my own blue music folder lying before me on the desk, I suddenly jerked when the room shriveled to a broom closet dusty quiet. There was only the soft shuffle of kids taking their seats.

Looking up, I smiled and took in a deep breath, along with an air of one in control, wearing the guise that there was something of importance that I wanted to discuss with them. I strolled to the front, pulled out a chair, and sat.

Positive now, I remarked brightly, "Well now, sounds like you all had a nice weekend. Let's check in with one another."

What followed were several beats in the rhythm of awkward body language communication. If it had been huge beach balls, they would have bounced rudely onto the floor. I cleared my throat.

The soprano who usually liked to help said, "Do you want me to pass out the music, Mamma?"

Shaking my head, I answered, "Not yet."

Another bounce. And then, a baritone voice from the back made a statement that sounded more like a question. "Yeah, you mean, seeing as how for Thursday we already nailed that piece into our memory, don' need no music, right?"

It was true that I had told them Friday that they would only be using their folders as props. Crossing my arms, I said, "Over the weekend, I gave some serious thought on how much time we have spent practicing for this tiny performance. Thursday will be half a day out of our schedule...." Those remarks seemed to hang without a reference in the air between us.

This was not going to be easy. Their faces tensed. They knew trouble had moved in.

I spoke again, that time, not forcing a smile. "The thing is," I began, "I'm not sure we should be spending our efforts with putting all of our time into singing that single hymn at the hotel, carting over our risers, when we have a expansive Christmas program to get ready for...."

A tenor, jumping to his feet and pointing at me, interrupted my rambling. "They don't want us, isn't that it?" He held still as a stork waiting for the fish to move into the right position. The fish moved her hands to her face to steady the jolt. At once, as if rehearsed, they commenced spouting off, getting up from chairs and clamoring about. My eyes flooded, and all I could think about was not to blink because it would cause the tears to spill down my face. I froze in wide-eyed, blurred vision. I was somewhere down in the center of this big green box of my classroom.

But I was the teacher. I simply had to step out and take control. Pulling out onto my feet while swiping the wet from my cheeks, I told them to please take their seats this instant, as if their obeying this command would somehow make everything sane again.

"No," a soprano said, "No, we won't sit! We've been working hard for this performance. You wrote a special arrangement for just us! And now we all the sudden on the week of—learn that they don't want us! We're mad as hell, that's what!"

I raised my voice to be heard. "I expect you to be angry. I'm angry. I want you to know that, last Friday, I resigned from that bigoted club." I lowered and leveled my voice. "I'm so sorry, I had no idea the ladies would react the way they did."

"Oh sure, nothin' nasty round bout with 'da ladies' till the ladies found out the singers was us black asses." I opened my mouth but I couldn't speak.

One of the basses strolled across the room and came to lean at me as he spoke. "You're sorry. Do you know what that means to us? Let me tell you about <u>sorry</u>." The air was stagnant and thick. Having a spokesman, they began to take their seats to watch. "What is sorry is peoples like you," he said, staring into my face.

"Me? But...."

"Like you. People like you have been telling us we were going to get to do things for centuries." He glanced back to his peers, who nodded and repeated his words like a Greek chorus.

"Telling us, uh huh."

"Do things, yeah."

91

"Like you, uh huh, like you."

He swerved back at me and continued, this time stressing each word: "It doesn't happen. The problem here is that you don't know your own people. You don't understand how they are. We do."

A beach ball thud and bounce bounce and roll away.

Faintly heard from the chorus: "Don' know. Thas right."

With that, he frowned, spent of reprisal. He stuck both of his hands in his pockets and turned. Shouldering forward, he moved to a seat.

The tenor got up again. "Thas right," he said with the air of an ambassador, "We, I say, we... didn't think they would really have us, but you, yes lady, you were so sure that it was going to be all right." He let the heft of his words dissipate and filter into the chalky air. And then, he evened his tone. "We thought, maybe this time it will be different."

"...different," softly echoed.

How could I ever have hoped to hide the ugly truth from these young people? They had already inherited so much disappointing truth from their parents and grandparents' experiences. Why did I ever consider hiding what was really going on?

"I can't justify it," I said simply. "Apparently, I didn't know my people, didn't want to acknowledge. If I had checked them out in September, I would have resigned then, and would not have put you through this. I feel ashamed and rather stupid." I searched each of them individually until they looked me in the eyes.

"The only thing I am sure of now—is that my vision of what small thing your performance might have done to bring the black and white communities together was right. My judgment of reality and how I should operate within that reality was naive and wrong. Equality will come; but now, no, you will not read about our dismissal, or of my resignation, not in the smallest column on the last page of the newspaper." Their faces set like stones in a river. I had to give them more than that. "But believe me," I began, "this issue has made a difference in the movement toward a social justice. "Word will get around," I said. "Evil never wins in the long run" My eyes were full again. Humbly, I said, "I have learned lessons from this experience—and, from you." They remained stones, studying me. But honesty between us had cut the anger.

Finally, I added, "I also want you to know that if you want me to resign my position as your teacher, I am prepared do so today. You have every right not to trust me now."

The green hush hugged us in the question. We waited for the answer to make itself known. We waited together for some long stillness.

At length, the bell's jarring rattle shattered the invisible frame that held us.

An alto got to her feet about the same time that I stood. She looked to be back to her old self, striding over to me like a May queen. She laid a hand on my shoulder and grinned.

"Oh, we trust you Mamma. We just gonna have to look out for you a little bit better from here on out!" She turned back to the others. "Right?"

At that signal, they chuckled, clucked, and whispered back and forth. Collecting their belongings, they began to leave, not as lighthearted as they had come, but comfortable with the transaction of the hour, and droll about the irony in it, saying they would see me tomorrow.

The alto called back over her shoulder, "Isn't it neat that we have clean robes for the Christmas performance?"

I was overwhelmed and exhausted. Glad that the next period was lunch, I shut the door. Slowly, I began to remove "Thanksgiving Hymn" from the folders, piling the sheets in a stack to file away before the end of the day.

The Christmas program went well. February found us busy with the Black History Month's showcase. Other departments joined the choir. Dramatics, drums, and dances took us from a campfire in Africa to the "Freedom March" in Alabama.

There was a rumble of opposition to the rumor that Lucy Addison, the heart of the African-American community, was to be shut down. A committee of basses and altos came to warn me that if trouble seemed inevitable, they would let me know, with ten minutes time to grab my purse and leave the school. Their concern was an act of respect. They told me they would not be able to protect me in a riot.

The day before the February show, the tenors suggested that I might be more comfortable directing the event from the side stage curtains. "That way, you'll be closer to us on stage, and maybe you hadn't thought of it, but our whole community comes out for this show." I understood. A favorite joke among them, when someone asked for me, was, "Hey man, don' you know she stand out in a crowd?"

The Black community had asked: How it could be easier to close a perfectly good high school than simply draw lines of integration where they should naturally fit? We heard no reasonable answer to that.

My husband and I had found out in March that our third child was on the way. I had let the administration know that I couldn't return in the fall. But I left the first of May. After a miscarriage, I was unable to return. My mentor shop teacher assured me that the students knew that stress was not a factor.

Lucy Addison was closed permanently in 1970. Its students were bussed across town to two integrated high schools.

Honorable Mention - Alphabetic Order
Wendy Bilen
Maryland

Wendy Bilen is the author of the award-winning biography-memoir *Finding Josie.* She earned an MFA in creative nonfiction from George Mason University, and her essays, articles, and photography have appeared in several newspapers and journals. The Ragdale Foundation and the DC Commission on the Arts and Humanities have also recognized her work. She lives in the Washington, DC, area where she teaches writing at the women's college of Trinity Washington University.

On the Range

The first time a gun goes off, my body jerks as if on strings. I am wearing the issued muffs, but the sound shoots from barrel to target, scattering across the concrete and back into my head. Stacey and I look at each other. The shots continue, one after another, and I twitch and jump, live with nerves.

We are colleagues, professors of English and psychology. We have come to this gun range because Stacey purchased a Groupon, and because our marriages have disintegrated, mine beyond mending. The husbands know we have come. We do not talk it up online or take pictures, conscious of how it could look, what it could imply, now or at any point in the future: evidence of that which does not exist.

Stacey's husband plans to move out. My husband is already gone, having moved seven hundred miles back to Chicago. The marriage has wilted me. I no longer recognize my voice. I question my decisions, leaning on my shopping cart for minutes in the supermarket while I debate which brand of sliced cheese to buy.

I had trouble finding the range, which lies nestled within an industrial park outside Washington, DC, next to a marsh with a noticeable absence of wildlife. I pulled into a spot facing the marsh and turned off the car. Immediately the muffled popping of gunfire poked holes in the silence. I caught peripheral movement through the passenger window, men and women hoisting large firearm cases over their shoulders, and wondered: who are these people?

Stacey had not yet arrived, but concerned about looking suspicious I opted to wait inside. I remember the building as corrugated metal, even as a dull yellow, but neither is right. It was straight up grey concrete, which makes more sense on every level. The door, black and off-center, seemed disproportionately small, squinty, as if whispering, *psssst, over here.*

Inside, the surprising space and unsurprising sterility of a warehouse. Muted fluorescent light, the kind that reveals every imperfection, hung suspended over rows of glass counters in a digital configuration. I wandered as if shopping at Tiffany's, entranced but not daring to linger, badge holders and gun cleaners and lock pickers rather than gold pendants and engravable key chains. Target choices lined the wall: zombies, pigs, mobsters. Near the door, cheap plastic chairs remained where customers had left them after sharing a Coke from the machine and maybe a show-and-tell over cheap plastic tables. A strange amalgamation, this place. Mostly it reminded me of pavilions at the fair, where 4-H members display their prize pigs and hand-sewn dresses and the sweet greasy smell of funnel cakes drifts in from outside.

I stated my vow in a rose garden north of Chicago on an overcast September afternoon, slow and emphatic, meaning every word, after the ceremony reinforcing the having and holding with, 'Let's never mention divorce.' I had been divorced. I have routinely told people that my first husband left me for another woman, a story true but oversimplified. I loved him. Everyone loved him. We spent nine years together—high school, college, his graduate school—and then he informed me by the glow of the Christmas tree that the status of our marriage had become *to be determined.* After weeks of this indecision, gutted, I demanded he move out, a charade intended to halt the madness, draw out the reassurance that he would never leave, and melt us back together. Instead he called my bluff, using my desperation as the running start toward freedom, and, as it turned out, another married woman. Admittedly I had not been an easy partner. I had problems; I got depressed. But he was studying to be a therapist, and I kind of believe that if anyone should have understood, it was him.

When I crawled out from the dark tangle of grief that had nearly persuaded me not to return, I recalibrated. I don't need all the romance, I told myself. I just need someone to walk through life with. I don't need—don't want—a handsome or popular man who might be lured away by a sweeter smile, sharper wit, kinder heart.

I lacked experience at dating casually. During eight years of high school and college I had dated exactly two boys and married one of them. A hopeless believer in lost causes, I felt great distress at ending any relationship once it started. If someone chose me, I was all but doomed.

Into this flimsiness stumbled the anti-ex-husband. Though he had eight years on me, words tripped out of him without the crescendos or decrescendos of social convention, and he didn't seem to notice or care. A purist, he read widely and could dialogue intelligently on the Grateful Dead, the stock market, Hemingway, foreign policy, or wiring an electrical switch. He had been a Marine, had worked in construction, politics, and finance. He laid out his career goal: to redevelop communities from within the banking industry. He gave without reservation to the homeless, volunteered whole Saturdays to charity building projects, wore unraveling sweaters to parties. Worldly, sandpapery, benevolent, an enigma—and he wanted me. Fascinated and flattered, I let myself be drawn in even as I reached for the glue.

Stacey handed over the Groupon. A chunky twentysomething with a buzz cut and a square peg through his earlobe set the gun and a box of bullets down, pivoting quickly, almost as if slinging a burger and fries. With a counter at shoulder height, the revolver lay inches from my face. A Taurus .38 Special. It surprised me with its long round barrel and curved wood handle, a prop that belonged in the hands of Clint Eastwood.

Brandon picked the gun back up, turning it over in his hands as he talked us through its anatomy. He clicked open the chamber, spun it, stopped it. After shaking a few shiny brass bullets from the box, he showed us how to slide them in. This gun, he noted, has no safety. Stacey and I exchanged a look.

Over in the practice booth, an imitation of things to come, he showed us how to stand. Plant your feet shoulder width apart. Lock your elbow so that the shot travels up your arm. Look through the sights, one in the middle, two on the outside. Many women like to cock the hammer halfway, which makes shooting easier. What most people aren't used to, he emphasized, is the sound.

In my hands the weight of the revolver makes it feel more real than any toy I've ever held, much more than a blue squirt gun that spews icy water from the hose or a cap gun loaded with dotted paper lines or grey plastic molded to look like metal for boys playing war. This is the temptress for stewing minds and idle hands, the destroyer of lives.

Armed guards and sharpshooters stand watch over important people at important sites not far from where I live and work: outside the White House, atop the Capitol, in motorcades of black SUVs. Neither semiautomatic handguns strapped to the belts of city law enforcement officers nor M-16s resting on the hips of Secret Service surprise me anymore, but my eyes still travel down to the weapon.

The odd reality: guns are everywhere and nowhere. I look but don't touch, so they stay familiar and foreign, someone else's power. I don't think of it as power, and I like to believe that if someone pulled a gun on me, I would not be afraid. (*What can man do to me?*) But I have been shaken by far less, so such an assumption collapses under its naiveté. I could have the power if I wanted it, but I don't want it. I don't want a gun in my house, don't want to go hunting, don't want to use one, ever, so why did I volunteer to come with Stacey, and why do I think that shooting a gun will make me feel better?

I recognized early in my second marriage, within weeks, that *union* was optimistic and talked myself out of the feelings of rejection my new husband's partitions evoked in me. So he closes the door to the bathroom. So he insists on folding his own laundry, buying his own deodorant and toothpaste. I considered these partitions cardboard symptoms of adjustment, those of a bachelor over forty, from a reserved Scandinavian family, a man who had lived alone for a long time. Surely they would bend and tear and eventually go out with the trash.

In some ways he employed the saccharine and superficial cuteness of early courtship, and in others, shifted into low idle. As if on cue, compliments stopped almost completely, except in cards adorned with bears and hearts on birthdays and anniversaries and Valentine's Day. He recoiled at my hands on his shoulders, touching me only when he wanted sex. He refused to shelve his books with mine, would not let me make his lunch for work, often talked to the dog more than he talked to me. Instead of relaxing into each other, we retained a terse, tense formality. I could not understand why our lives weren't merging and sobbed without sound, clutching the sheet in the dark as his breathing slowed and he fell asleep.

Efforts to talk it through ended badly. He felt attacked, engulfed by overly high expectations, and I felt I had not loved him enough.

I remembered a conversation in his garden apartment before we married. His parents concerned me, I said. I had cringed at the relationship between his mother, so fragile, nearly apologizing for her existence, and his father, who barked at her and repeated the same few stories on an endless loop. I did not want to end up with a marriage like theirs: silent, seemingly strained.

'That's not going to happen,' he had said.

At our house in Northeast DC, I sometimes heard gunshots. I tried to convince myself they were firecrackers, maybe, or something automotive. But I had seen the squad cars speeding down our street, a blur of blue and red, and had caught the stories in the *Post*. My husband came to loathe that house, DC, and the East Coast, longing to return to the Midwest. We loved Illinois, home to us both for most of our lives, but left shortly after getting married simply because we wanted to do something different. I got homesick first, but he convinced me to wait it out, to move from the suburbs in Virginia to the city itself. We bought a fixer-upper. I finished an MFA and graduated with a full-time college teaching job and book contract in hand.

In his way, he had supported me during the long process of discovering my life's work and supported me still, though inconsistently and with methods I could not understand. He would research something I mentioned during dinner or be quick to help with questions that arose as I wrote, but I received no word of congratulations or hug when I met him on the front step with the first copy of my book. He would buy my favorite Italian chocolates just because, leaving them in a drawer or on the counter, but frequently he would not acknowledge me when I walked into the house after we had been apart for a day or longer.

I had theories.

The house. The house had launched a full attack, cracking, spouting water, sinking, and revealing secrets that revealed more secrets, all of which involved work that we did ourselves. In the evenings and on weekends, we hammered, mudded, painted, and tiled, dragging carloads of plaster to the dump.

His job. He had reached his mid-forties and still held positions that did not allow him to fulfill his passion for rebuilding communities. He was working his way there, he said, but since I met him he had been through at least ten jobs. Each one started with promise, but when *They don't know what they're doing* surfaced during dinner, I knew it was a matter of time.

Our news. I could not have children.

The common denominator: me.

Let's take a break from the house, I said, or even pay someone. Normal people pay people. Get a job you want, I said. Take the pay cut. We'll figure it out. He would not entertain this reasoning. He still would not let me get him a soda from the refrigerator.

The same frustrations that stirred dissatisfaction within him bound me to that place. An inverse correlation, my colleagues tell me. Yes, we tore the second floor down to its studs, but we built it back up again. Despite faltering my way through the first few semesters, politically and pedagogically, I had the chance every day to instill confidence, life skills, and value in dozens of under-resourced young women as I taught them how to write. Sometimes they ignored me, resisted, and/or disappeared, but some tried, and some learned. I knew that I was doing something very important, and I was good at it. I felt myself settle into the house and the city. For the first time in years, I felt anchored, and for the first time in my life, I didn't think of my job as a job. I felt alive. Free. When I lived in Illinois, restaurants and streets and parks—nearly everything, really—reminded me of what I had lost. Here, North Capitol Street and the gelato at the National Gallery belonged not to my ex-husband, not to my ex-marriage, but to me, and to my now-life, a life crafted from perseverance.

We worked on our house and edged toward adopting a child through the DC foster care system. We drove downtown for training sessions with other would-be foster parents, rolled our fingers for prints, completed long questionnaires (*How likely are you to take a child with fetal alcohol syndrome?*), did whatever needed doing to be someone's forever family.

On 08.08.08 an eleven-year-old girl moved in. Lanky, sassy, clingy, and moody, she had problems. I still believed in the possibility of my marriage, but problems + problems = more problems. Instead of seeing her behaviors for what they were, the inclinations of a very troubled child, my husband took them personally. He said he needed to see more improvement. She said she wanted another father. He set a deadline. She didn't meet it. She wanted out. He said to give it to her. I knew she didn't want out. I knew exactly what she wanted because I had wanted the same thing from both of my husbands: to hear the words, 'I love you more than I can say, and I'm not going anywhere.'

Another problem: I saw her as my daughter, and I did love her more than I could say.

He made me choose: him or her. Because she was not legally our daughter yet, I couldn't choose her—take a still-foster child and leave my husband?—so I went along with his argument that she didn't want to live with us, and she left after nine months. When she drove away with the social worker, part of me and a big part of my marriage dragged along behind the van, the remains mangled and unrecognizable.

During a momentary pause in the shooting, Stacey and I open the black metal door and carry our .38 Special, box of bullets, and complimentary targets into the range, looking for booth 11. The frigid air startles me. On the walls, black foam in a parquet pattern. On the floor, a steel grate over a concrete pit, alive with the gleam of bullet casings. White noise seems to fill the headphones that aren't headphones, like the far-off sound of the sea in a shell.

Three men in booth 12 begin firing semi-automatic handguns. I cannot see them fully because of the partial walls, but I see enough to know they do not flinch. I cannot stop flinching. I focus on their paper target, some ten yards away, and watch the holes appear. The black silhouette turns into a sieve. Casings fly into our booth, bouncing off the counter and the walls with a steady echo: bass, treble.

Unfamiliar and a little disoriented, we peer and twist, deducing and concluding so that we can do the work we have come to do. We spot a small digital box on the wall and tentatively press one of the buttons. The holder flies toward us.

We clip the target to the holder and press another button. The target rushes away, trying to keep up.

Stacey goes first. She hits above the shoulder. She pauses, considers, looks back at me, and then fires again. Still too high. The gun pulls her arms upward with the recoil.

Watching her, I think of Brian Turner's poem, 'Here, Bullet.' I remember the scene in 'Salvador' when Joan Didion reaches into her purse on a deserted sidewalk and suddenly hears the cocking of guns up and down the street. I think of the boy in *96 Minutes* who uses the power of a gun to avoid paying for his chips, of *Unforgiven*, when Clint Eastwood really is holding a prop.

I think about people who live with this sound, without headphones, and the nervous silence in between: soldiers, civilians, some of my students. In my head swirl images of children hypnotized by a screen, their faces contorting and their hands an intense orchestration of *staccato* and *presto* (points for death).

Stacey hands the gun to me.

He didn't want to talk about losing our child. As I sat crumpled in tears, the marriage counselor, visibly exasperated, said to him, 'Can't you come alongside her as she grieves?' He had no idea what that meant.

It's not that he *wouldn't* do these things I expected, he said, but that he *couldn't*. He *couldn't* ask about my life, respond to my touch, grieve with me—and *couldn't* change. A good man, who loved me, who couldn't do the things required to develop intimacy in a marriage: it's not that I *wouldn't* but that .I *couldn't* understand.

He lost his job. He left our church. After eighteen months, despite my protests, he took a position in Chicago. We could adopt, he said, if I left my teaching job and my church, and my friends, and our home. He would not negotiate. Everything in DC had come to represent all that was wrong with our marriage, that which had soured and poisoned us. We had planned to leave DC, but that was before. I didn't want to let go of my work or my home without a child—for whom I now knew I would go anywhere. Now he placed before me another choice: my marriage or my life's work, a family or my home. I didn't know if I could believe him when he said a child was forthcoming.

For another year and a half, I stayed in DC while I tried to find a life for myself in Chicago. I prayed, wondered if I was being selfish, looked for every possible way to keep gripping that which was slipping away again. But *he couldn't*. Somehow the responsibility of the decision, like a grenade, tossed, still landed at *my* feet. I did not want to hurt him, to end another marriage, to effectively leave someone when I knew what it was like to have someone leave me. Friends, family, pastors, and coworkers said to me, 'But Wendy, *he* left.' That somehow did not add up to enough.

Broken, I finally said no more and pulled the trigger.

Gun raised before me, I peer down the barrel, which leads to the target like an estuary to the sea. As I line up the sights, my body tenses, knowing, and I curl my finger until the trigger gives. The force races up my arms to my shoulders, the tiny explosion of powder and metal powerful and, for the moment, in control.

The first time I shoot, I hit the heart. Twice.

I shoot again, again, again, losing track of how many bullets I have left. The barrel heats and sends up a thread of smoke. I get worse instead of better, aiming low and hitting high.

There is only the target, the gun, and me. It seems surreal, childish, a small, desperate fusion of wood and steel, and I feel nothing but a terrible awareness of the power in my grip.

I want to keep shooting, but I also want the noise to stop.

The noise does stop when we run out of bullets and when I inform the judge there is no hope for reconciliation.

I tell my husband, 'All I wanted was you.'

He replies, 'You had me.'

I believe in a God with power far greater than our need, but that power has not worked in my marriage. Twice. Of course not: power cannot coexist with love. Despite all this talk of women's rights and American dreams, I cannot will a man to know me or pray him into staying. The first time, I gave myself so completely that I nearly died when he left. The second time, I nearly died because I stayed. I morphed into something I could not recognize, my self pushed down and hid, corseted, the me who had not had a chance to become. My life, a loaded gun that stood in the corner until they came and carried me away.

You can't unshoot a gun, unhear the noise, unpierce the target. You can forgive. You can choose to hold hope close, to survive, to avoid turning the gun on yourself.

Honorable Mention - Alphabetic Order
Colleen Lutz Clemens
Pennsylvania

Colleen Lutz Clemens is the editor of several books of non-fiction including *Philadelphia Reflections: Stories from the Delaware to the Schuylkill and* has published short essays in various collections such as *Click: When We Knew We Were Feminists.* Her work on miscarriage and infertility has been published in the magazine *TRIVIA* and the collection *Three Minus One.* She writes about writing, mothering, and culture for *Scary Mommy, Literary Mama, Noodle, bitchflicks,* and *feministing.* Colleen lives in Bucks County, PA, with her partner, dogs, and daughter and can be reached via her blog kupoco.wordpress.com.

Breath by Breath

I was doing grown-up things before I was really a grown-up. At the age of 23, I started teaching English to high school seniors. At 24, I was married and we bought our house. I found myself ill, unable to sleep, incapable of shutting down the thoughts in my head. I worried about money, our dog, my husband, the house, the laundry, my sister, the world, women everywhere, my students. Worries were making me sick.

I worked out hard, pushing myself on a spin bike or forcing myself to run on the treadmill before school. I was lean, looked healthy, but never felt that way. I ran on adrenaline and sugar, reaching for the candy in my desk by sixth period. After her mother died too early from ovarian cancer, the librarian at my school invited me to a yoga class. Though I had little interest, she and her partner were attending in search of some calm, so I decided to try along with them.

At first, we sat on the gym's yoga mats and breathed. I was bored. Irritated. I felt like I wasn't doing anything productive. My mind wandered as it always did; I peeked at the clock. The weights banging to the floor in the next room irked me. Drips of sweat from the previous spinning class scented the floor next to my nose.

We began to move through the poses. Fortunately, the instructor didn't use Sanskrit. If she did, I wouldn't have gone back the next week. Her throaty voice piped over the speakers, asking us to get on our knees and move like an angry cat. I felt no challenge.

Then she brought us into pigeon.

At first, I didn't understand what she wanted us to do. I looked at people's shins running parallel to the front of their mats and tried to emulate them. Though my legs didn't cooperate, I lay my chest to the floor. My forehead rested on the borrowed mat, and tears welled up in my eyes. My hip felt warm, soft. I felt like I was home and didn't need to worry about bills and grading and all of the other thoughts that usually felt so important.

Ten years later, pigeon remained my favorite pose. I added it to my practice even when the instructor didn't take us there because it offered me the solace others find on a meditation cushion or during a long run. Pigeon became a necessity.

ॐ

My husband Matt and I didn't sit at home pining for the child we wanted. During our marriage's first ten years, we traveled, worked on our house, and did graduate work. Then we paused: I was 32 and hadn't been able to conceive. We were going to need help.

During a January snowstorm we drove the half-hour to the fertility clinic. We called ahead to make sure the office was open. We didn't yet know the fertility world does not—cannot—stop for anything, especially not something so silly as inclement weather. The doctor had a cold, her desk littered with unread medical journals and patient files. Her purple velour outfit was outdated. I immediately loved her, saw her as one of my people: creative and organized in her own way, able to make something from nothing, as I hoped she would do with me.

Our treatments began. Feeling like we had little time to waste, we skipped Clomid—an easier but less effective pill—and chose the more aggressive treatment of Bravelle injections.

Our vocabulary grew. *Subcutaneous. Follicles. Progesterone.* While writing my dissertation, inky papers and stained napkins strewn about my regular table at the coffee shop, my mind wandered to the baby I hoped would soon grow inside me.

Matt and I began to drown in the fertility world, a space where everything sexy becomes sterile and all of one's private parts become public. Sex was regulated by a calendar. Matt often complained about the lack of privacy he felt when giving his "sample."

But even "expressing" a specimen into a Dixie cup in a bright, noisy clinic paled in comparison to the immodesty necessary for a woman's survival in the world of reproductive medicine. My private life became other people's business. Before entering the clinic for my daily blood draw, I left a small treat—a cookie, a chocolate—on the dash as a reward for my bravery. If I saw my favorite phlebotomist was not working, I cringed to imagine another stranger taking my blood. My yoga breathing kept me calm as I extended my small-veined, bruised arm.

My stomach, firm and strong from yoga, became another bloodied battleground where my husband injected me with hormones. At $100 a shot, we watched our savings dwindle. During intrauterine inseminations cycles, I endured what I called "wanding," where a nurse probed my insides to measure my uterine lining and count my eggs as I tried to convince one of them to make a zygote. Nothing about my body was my own anymore. I had given it over to science, put my trust in the doctor who could make the baby we couldn't make on our own.

అ✦ఈ

That February, we got pregnant from our first IUI cycle. My nurse Joyce called to tell us the news, which we shared with immediate family and close friends. We had achieved our goal. I carried the secret with me for days, smiling to myself with the early knowledge of a life growing rapidly inside. I continued to go the office for blood draws.

A few days later Joyce called again. My hormone levels weren't multiplying, a signal that my body wasn't going to maintain the pregnancy. I didn't understand then that there is no magical reversal for this lack of multiplication. The numbers weren't in my favor; the baby wasn't going to stay. On a Saturday morning, I sat in the doctor's office where she explained over and over that there was nothing I could do.

అ✦ఈ

Because my body and mind were consumed by fertility treatments, I threw myself into my yoga practice. I came to the mat several times a week in search of a quiet mind and a body receptive to a baby. I graduated to a yoga studio where the mystical elements of yoga didn't have to yield to the physical elements emphasized at the gym. My own mat became my sanctuary, a space where I could wash my mind of worry and sadness and allow my body to counteract the hormones entering it.

Pigeon became even more special to me, as it asked me to surrender in my hips, the place that felt most violated. My shin now ran parallel to the front edge of my mat, thanks to years of practicing. My hips sat squared to the floor. I welcomed the warm rush the pose gave my back and legs. My forehead kissed the ground, and I imagined my concerns seeping into Mother Earth. I released the anxiety I held over the fertility treatments and the loss. I could have stayed there all day. My breath slowed. My jaw slackened. Pigeon allowed me to rest, offered me the ease in my body I no longer felt.

I lost the first baby in February. In May a breast cancer scare resulted in a benign diagnosis. A week later I graduated with my PhD and delivered the commencement address to thousands of people. In June I started teaching yoga at a local studio. Matt and I were taking a break from the fertility world, as it was putting too much pressure on our marriage. Too many of our conversations were about loss, medicines, and money; we had lost ourselves in our ambitions and needed to step away from them.

రావ∽6

Then in July we miraculously got pregnant on our own. We heard the baby's magical heartbeat the week before our tenth anniversary. I sent a text message to my best friend: "Heartbeat strong." At our celebration dinner, we envisioned our next ten years as we raised our child. When I went to the bathroom upstairs at the inn, I heard an owl outside the window. The next day we went to the doctor for our week seven ultrasound and heard only the deafening sound of a heartbeatless room.

I had to take another break from the fertility treadmill. In July I had the D and C, my friend who had one years before

117

called it a "scoop and suck," and threw myself into my new role as a professor in August.

Nine months later, we felt ready to try another IUI cycle. Two weeks later I got my period. It hadn't worked. All of our efforts from those almost three years started to seem futile. Thoughts of the baby I might never have consumed me. Our marriage felt tender and frail.

The next summer, I was offered a full time, tenure track position, and for a moment I felt grateful the IUI cycle hadn't taken. Now I could focus on my career, something I was good at, something that made sense, that I could control.

We decided to try IUI one last time. If it didn't take, we would have to decide whether to go deeper into the fertility world and try in vitro fertilization, take the route of adoption, or give up all together. I relied on my yoga practice even more, using the time to visualize my womb as a warm and open space, focusing light and energy on my root chakra, and working with my personal mantra: *Breath by breath I will bring you into being.* My practice had taught me that the only thing I could do to help bring my child into this world was breathe and be present. I needed to surrender even more in my poses. As I sank into a deep, rich, warm pigeon that undid the stresses of the injections, pokings, and proddings, I found relief. I know the other students in the room greeted pigeon with a groan, but I welcomed it like an old friend who could always make me laugh, even in the darkest moments.

❧❧

The cycle worked. Matt and I tried not to hold our breath and attempted to go about our daily routines. I hid my nausea from my colleagues, students, and friends. I could not endure telling the world for a third time that we had lost a baby, so we only told our closest circle of friends. My fingers clenched the steering wheel as I drove to my weekly ultrasound appointments. I lived in fear of silence, not only from the lack of a heartbeat, but from the pause that occurs the moment when I can already tell from the doctor's face that she will give me bad news.

My fear grew as the seventh week approached. I didn't believe I could recover from another loss. I feared this was my last chance to have we dreamed of, that at any moment this little being could be lost. *Breath by breath*, I reminded myself. That Friday morning we saw the baby's heart flicking like a tiny fingernail on the screen. We heard it. We had made it further than we ever had before.

I started the next day like every other Saturday: on my mat. My fears led me to the bathroom every twenty minutes to make sure I wasn't bleeding. I was working on trusting my body, trusting that things would work out. Late in the class, we began our hip openers. I brought my right shin to the front of the mat, slid my left leg back. The back of my heart melted. I turned my cheek to the floor and released the tension in my neck. The relief of seeing the baby on the monitor the day before washed over my body and mind. I breathed in the possibility of the little one coming in a few months.

Then I felt like I had to go to the bathroom. I told myself that it was okay, that—just like every other time—I was overreacting, that I couldn't allow fear to overtake my life. But something felt different. My focus lost, I rose from my mat and went to the bathroom for the third time during the class.

I was bleeding. The bright red blood every pregnant woman fears. I left the bathroom, put on my shoes but not my socks, left my mat unrolled on the floor, and fled the studio. By the time I arrived at the hospital, my car seat was stained with what I believed to be my third lost pregnancy.

ॐॐ

This time the baby stayed. I had a subchorionic hematoma; my placenta tore away from my uterus. Again we saw her flickering heart, heard the strength already inside of her. I was put on bed rest. My terror mounted. I knew I wanted her, needed her. Almost losing her showed me just how much.

Once allowed to return to yoga, I had to face those fears and uncertainties. I was tentative on my mat, unable to trust the thing in which I had put my faith for a decade. Returning to my practice—the only place that had offered me quiet in a loud, loud life—scared me. My fear seemed irrational; yoga had not caused the tear. But the tear showed itself when I was prostrate on my mat, where I had allowed myself to be vulnerable over and over again for ten years and where I felt safe in that vulnerability.

Now pigeon offered neither safety nor comfort. For most yogis I know, going into pigeon is the epitome of discomfort, but for me *not* going into it was the discomfort. I no longer looked forward to hearing the music slow for our hip series. Instead at every practice I found myself facing the terror of losing my baby. While everyone else squirmed in pigeon, I watched with jealousy. But I refused to go into the pose that I felt in some way caused my baby distress.

I grew irritated and angry with myself for letting such an irrational fear overtake me. But still I showed up for my practice, knew it was good for me and the baby to move and breathe together. She and I grew bigger, and our practice evolved, grew slower and more fluid. I came to trust in her just as much as I trusted in myself. I repeated *Breath by breath, I will bring you into being.* When the time for pigeon came, the anger eventually subsided because I realized pigeon would always be there. The practice is thousands of years old. I could be kind to my mind—even if it didn't make sense to my intellect—and give myself a few months of skipping pigeon. I regarded this kindness to myself as my daughter's first lesson in compassion. I was showing up for the practice, the hardest part of yoga. I was allowed to make choices based on emotion in the name of protecting myself and my daughter.

I used those few minutes of each class, everyone else's face to the mat, to breathe life into my baby. Breath by breath, breath by breath she came into being.

Colleen Lutz Clemens

122

Honorable Mention - Alphabetic Order
Kristin Leclaire
Colorado

Kristin Leclaire's nonfiction has appeared *Literary Mama* and *The Bohemyth*, and she recently won the Denver Stories on Stage flash fiction contest. One of her essays last spring made the *Masters Review* shortlist and was a finalist for the Annie Dillard Award for creative nonfiction. This year four of her essays will appear in print anthologies, including a new book by Creative Nonfiction called *Becoming a Teacher*. She teaches high school English and lives in Littleton, Colorado with her husband and two toddlers.

Kristin Leclaire

Inside the Labyrinth

I read a story once by Jorge Luis Borges about a magical library. Sunlight streamed through its cathedral ceilings, comforting the bowed heads of its patrons. This library's collection was infinite. The towering shelves formed a labyrinth, housing books with every possible combination of letters, even when the words were not really words at all. Rather, the letters sprayed across white pages like little bullets, riddling the books with inky marks no one could explain or understand. Some readers never found their way out.

At least, that's what I think the story was about. I read it in its original Spanish with only my hole-punched worksheets of vocabulary and irregular verb conjugations. Also, it was existential, so its meaning likely escaped me. But when I opened the yellowed pages of that Spanish book, I found my sixteen-year-old self leaning against a tower of leather-bound, nutmeg-smelling pages. My body was trying to translate the story for me.

Now, as a high school English teacher in Littleton, Colorado, I am the ultimate translator. I translate the scratches of sophomore boys into essays about Daedalus and Icarus. I translate the eye roll of the girl in the third row into her breakup with the basketball player in the fifth row. I translate, with a giggle, group work evaluations that state, "This project sucked. Largely because one of our members was *incontinent*." This was in response to a question about the group's overall *competence*. I translate dreamy run-on sentences of a sixteen-year-old boy pining away for a girl with "the face of an angle." I write, "Best to measure that kind of beauty with a protractor" in the margins of his three-page memoir.

Lately, I've been translating nervous glances to the lock on the classroom door every time someone shuts a locker too hard. These glances ask, "Are we safe?" So I test the door handle, right before returning to our discussion of Steinbeck with a little nod they translate as, "Yes, you are safe. I will keep you safe."

I walked back into the Arapahoe High School library yesterday after being shut out for six months. Even its windows were blacked over, like mirrors cloaked in mourning, as its insides endured evisceration. It's not open yet to students, but the other teachers and I have been encouraged to walk through and make peace with it. Most things have found their new places. The old carpet, rubbed from fifty years of soles, is gone. It and its bloodstains were ripped out before the memorial services took place. The new carpet's fibers are stiff and bright. Not a footprint to be found. The stuffed chairs have gone, too, and pencil marks from decades of daydreaming boys and girls have been erased. The countertops are so black and sleek that everything seems to slide right off them, and the chairs are hard. I don't know where to sit down.

⇛⇝

In our old Arapahoe library, we'd walk through the glass doors, past the Arapahoe Indian statue watching over us, and into an alphabetical display of new hardback books with shiny protective covers and spines not yet broken. I'd make extra trips to the library in the last week of October, partly to peruse the annual pumpkin contest, partly to help myself to the candy corn and hot apple cider that Louisa, the librarian's assistant, laid out for us teachers in the back. Louisa wore black cat and orange pumpkin sweaters on Halloween and jingle bell earrings in December. When I jammed the copy machine, she'd rip out the paper tray with a deep sigh, but her voice was low and the soft crinkles reaching out from her eyes and lips gave her a permanent grandmother smile. Next to the buzzing copy machine, wafts of cinnamon steam curled out of the silver urn she'd brought for the cider.

Everyone and everything in the library was buzzing; the DECA girls clacking out their business presentations on the old Dells, two boys from my third hour doing algebra homework and sneaking Doritos from their backpacks, the Spanish teacher chatting with the head librarian, Tracy Murphy, while hacking away flashcards on the paper cutter. It was the buzz of energy, of things getting checked off to-do lists. It was a lullaby on Mondays, a hymn on Fridays.

Didn't we kind of grow up in a library? It was the sacred place of sing-songy storytime and round carpets, the place where we fell in love with our teachers and lost our first teeth, where walls were made of books and "READ" posters. As the teacher turned each page, we'd lean in, and lean in a little more until we could breathe her right in. We'd swing from one bold print word to another like they were monkey bars. We could sit with bare legs sprawled on a steam-cleaned carpet, tongues poking out and backs relaxed into bows.

As a little girl I'd spend the summer wandering the infinite bookcases of our white-pillared neighborhood library. While my third-grade friends attended morning mass and Jewish summer camp, I went to the Tremont Library in Old Arlington, a leafy suburb of Columbus, Ohio. I rode my bike under the green canopies of tree-lined, asphalt roads where old

Ohio farms had transformed into red-bricked suburban homes with circle driveways. The Tremont Library rested in a sleepy neighborhood, its fire lane often occupied by moms in tennis skirts and gold earrings, dropping off their kids' books on the way to swim meets.

I'd stroll through the glass doors and approach the chestnut altar of the old card catalogue. I loved sliding out those smooth, narrow drawers, each card inside neatly charting the facts of a book's life. The cards were closely packed, and I grazed their tops with the palm of my hand as though I were stroking the soft bumps of my cat's spine. The Challenger had exploded, I'd failed my fraction test, my best friend was already sporting a training bra, and my piano teacher taught me the word "mediocre" by using it to describe my talent, but here at the Tremont Library, the Dewey Decimal system ruled all. Here, the world made sense.

After this brief worship, I'd head for the mystery shelf in the young adult room, past the Nancy Drews and right to the Trixie Beldens. Trixie was a bold, curly-haired girl who solved mysterious misdeeds in her small town's caves and manors. The scariest moments were only scary enough to keep me reading, and the climax of each story quickly resolved into a sensible ending: the ghost was just a peeved maid, the vampire a disgruntled heir, and the monster an angry boy.

I touched each book, fingering diamond dust jackets and pages edged with red ink, and stared back at Trixie's wide, doll-like eyes on the peeling 1950s covers. I'd pull out the story I wanted, check it out with the library card in my jean pocket, and ride home with it in my backpack. With an orange cat curled up on my tan feet and a pretzel rod dangling from my lips, I'd turn pages until Trixie's tomboyish hands were mine. The dankness of the haunted mansion dampened the skin on my arms. The clues--a frayed photo, tidbits of overheard conversation, shadowy sightings--were laid out before me, and I assembled them like a puzzle. Each mystery was solved. Good people got shiny medals while villains often turned out not to be villains at all. And Trixie and I saw it all coming from a mile away. There were no press releases, no SWAT team masks and guns, ordering us to "get your hands on your heads and fucking RUN." There were no fifteen-year-olds so terrified that they ran out of their shoes, dirty snow penetrating their naked feet.

If Trixie were here with me, would her wide eyes be able to see all of this? The two of us could lift up her wooden-handled magnifying glass and examine the evidence, all of it spattered among the police report, my memory, and retold stories. Help me, Trixie, translate these clues:

Fact 1: Karl drops off his little sister at school, nodding his blonde head when she says, "I'll see you after school" before closing the door.

Fact 2: Claire, a sleek-haired senior who loves horses, watches Karl barge through the glass doors, shotgun in his marked-up hands. She asks him, "What are you doing, Karl?" He answers her with three bullets.

Fact 3: In the English office, I put down my hot chocolate, log into my computer and hear three bangs from the barrel of a gun: black, hollow Os swallowing the hallways.

Fact 4: I crouch behind someone else's desk, using another teacher's phone to send a text to my husband: "This is Kristin. There has been a shooting at Arapahoe. I am ok." I don't believe a word of it.

Fact 5: My two tall boys from third hour eat and scratch out homework in the library when Karl enters, yelling, "Where the fuck is Murphy?" Bandoliers cross his chest, shells falling to the floor as he shoots at the front desk. His fantasy of murdering our librarian--the man who had cut him from the debate team earlier that year--slips away.

Fact 6: Max, one of my tall sophomore boys, bolts from the library. When he reaches the trophy hall, he pauses at the puddle of blood next to Claire, who now lies face down like a dropped doll.

Fact 7: Karl, after piercing the checkout desk with bullets and blackening the shelves with a homemade bomb, kills himself between shelves of e.e.cummings and Robert Frost.

Fact 8: Louisa, the librarian's assistant with jingle bell earrings, stands just outside the King Soopers we've been evacuated to, gripping an empty cart. She doesn't seem to hear me until I ask, "Did you see it?" She nods slowly, like a sleepwalker, brown eyes locked on something invisible to me.

Fact 9: The next day, students shiver in the cold, stuffing styrofoam cups into a chain link fence to spell out "Warrior Strong" before the candlelight vigil for Claire, who sleeps in a nearby hospital.

Fact 10: Between the snow and Christmas lights, my department chair sends us a text on the darkest evening of the year. Claire is dead. The vigil didn't work.

Fact 11: When the crime scene tape comes down, teachers return to the building for their cell phones, purses, and cars. The classrooms are just as we left them, except empty. Desks in neat rows of six hold up handouts and dead phones. The counselors have taken the liberty of closing the students' binders and books, and I wonder if Karl died with his eyes open or closed.

Fact 12: Karl's mom with gentle, shaky hands pulls out my chair for me as I try not to picture Karl in their now half-empty home, still partially decorated from Christmas. I am there to tutor the sister he's left behind.

Fact 13: Warm stickiness seeps from my temple into my pillow, turning from blood to tears as I wake up with Karl's body in my mind. He is still smoking from the gunshot, blood soaking into the library's floor.

❧❦

In our new Arapahoe library, these clues have been painted over, recarpeted, and sanded away. Now, I walk into a clean space of flat screens, TVs with scrolling announcements, and surge-protected outlets. The surviving books have migrated from the walls of the library to its heart. Small worlds still beat in between their covers, and I hear them even in the buzz of the high-tech group study rooms. Windows have replaced burned library shelves, and student volunteers shuffle old books onto new shelves. I'm not quite sure where to walk or if I'm allowed to sit down. Each time I turn, I bump into a glass wall.

There's one familiar corner: the glass case housing our Arapaho Indian statue. After the shooting, the Arapaho Indian tribe performed a cleansing of our library and the hallway where Claire was shot. The ceremony was private, but afterward I could smell the sweetness of burning sage in the spots most concentrated with death. I wondered if the tribal elders had stepped into the library to find Karl's ghost standing in the corner, the rage on his face slacked into confusion. He'd turned the library into a purgatory. I hoped that the sweeping motions of the Indians' feathers, fanning the sage higher and higher, had brushed his death off the book jackets and into the air outside.

Standing next to the new circulation desk, I try to imagine the DECA girls and the basketball boys strolling into this library, backpacks full of Spanish homework, Shakespeare plays, and energy drinks in tall black cans. I picture my sophomore boys typing their essays on laptops, giving them only a cursory glance before sharing them with me. Just down the hall with our office door wide open, other English teachers and I might find our way back to each other by reading aloud the funniest errors in our students' stories. Before the shooting, my deskmate liked to inform me that teenagers don't care to be "taken for granite," and I'd reply by wondering why so many seniors plan to spend the next four years in some kind of "collage." She'd always win, though, by asking me, "Who doesn't enjoy a soft, genital breeze from time to time?"

But my favorite, my very favorite, was the young memoirist who recently responded to a metaphor exercise with this sentence: "I am the clam before the storm."

I imagine my memoirist typing sentences like this one in the new library when it opens to students next week. She will chat, perhaps, with some student council kids at a high table in the library's café as school announcements scroll on the screen above her head. Throwing her bag on the ground, she'll stretch her arms into a sleepy yawn. I can see the rest of the kids in the new library lounging, too, arms thrown over the backs of chairs like they're sitting in their own living rooms. As she and her friends laugh and type homework and eat cookies from the school store, the air around them will quiver and lighten. The silent eye of the storm will pass into something noisier, and she will mistakenly trade her "calm" for a "clam." Sometimes lovely things come from mistakes. She will close her laptop case, open her planbook, and cross off "Get ready for tomorrow" with a wavy blue line.

My hand hovering above the checkout counter, I picture that tiny clam shivering on the foamy edge of the shore. I think of the clam as I feel my way back into the library. Heavy clouds move in, swallowing patches of blue sky with roars of thunder and singeing the ground with arrows of lightning. Nothing sounds or feels quite the same after the gunshots, and I move by groping, grasping, slumping against dead ends, rerouting. That clam could be washed out to the deep at any moment, uprooted and taken for a ride. Yet there it is, wobbling between the wet thickness of the sand and the disorienting rip of the tide, holding on even though there is little to hold onto.

I press my thumb onto the new circulation desk, softening the counter with my fingerprint. It forms a silvery spiderweb, or a delicate compass, depending on how the light catches it.

Honorable Mention - Alphabetic Order
Liz Lynch
New Jersey

Raised in Somerset County, New Jersey, Liz Lynch graduated Indiana University-Bloomington with a double degree in journalism and German. After spending more than a decade as an editor and reporter at several newspapers, including the Miami Herald, the Fort Lauderdale Sun-Sentinel and the Chicago Sun-Times, she now writes scripts, essays and articles as a freelancer. She lives in Montclair, New Jersey with her husband and two daughters.

(photo credit: Grace Brown)

Liz Lynch

Eighty-Three Books

The public library in my New Jersey suburb held a contest the summer I turned nine, the summer of '69. Whoever read the most books would win –

– Nothing specific, come to think of it. They just said we'd *win*, which was enough for me, third of seven children, restlessly jockeying to be noticed. I lived to be fastest, to answer quickest, to find the wishbone first. A contest – any contest – rang Pavlovian bells in my hot-wired brain. I could even feel virtuous about this one; it was *educational*

With a sawed-off pencil, I printed my name on the sheet as soon as they posted it, still scented with Magic Marker. I was a bright-eyed sprinter, crouched tight, waiting for the gun.

☞☜

At my house, if you could read, you were a library regular. Library Days were steady pulses in the lazy rhythm of our summers. We set out on bikes, kitted out in bright polyester shorts and tops from Two Guys on Route 22 (*home of low-LOW prices!*). We always tightened the leatherette straps securing our plastic bike baskets, knowing they'd sag alarmingly with the loads we piled inside.

Pedaling down our street, we'd pause in the long, cool Romanesque shadow of our parish church, and pause more nervously a half-block later at the Rubicon posed by the town's main drag, where a smelly stream of cars and trucks whizzed by unchecked until the county sprang for a stoplight fifteen years later. Braving that, we cruised past barking dogs and patchy stretches of privet hedge before parking on the white concrete in front of our brick box of a library.

Hurrying through the tan-and-orange lobby, we ran our hands down the thick walnut handrails of the stairs leading to the basement Children's Room, our holding pen until junior high. I envied my mother the freedom of the airy upstairs Adult Room. I envied even more the wallet-sized adult card that she *carried in her purse*, so unlike our clunky 3x5s, locked away in a Children's Room file cabinet.

෨৶ঌ

The summer contest had only one ironclad rule: We had to read at our grade level or above. Otherwise, we checked out books as usual (maximum: six, term: two weeks). Upon returning books, contestants filled out a slip of paper listing the titles. For every five books, we got a round blue sticker next to our names on a big chart on the Children's Room wall.

There were no limits on how much fiction or how much nonfiction; no rules about how long to wait before returning books. I'm not even sure the books *had* to come from the Children's Room, either (although we'd probably have tried driving our parents' cars before we'd ask to borrow an Adult Room book).

So, I could see but one directive: to read and read and read, gloating over the swelling regiment of blue stickers by my name. I was *made* for this contest. It required only what I already did every summer: hauling off armloads of books, devouring them, returning them like clockwork, ready to refuel.

మ~మ

The contest sparked mass excitement for a week or two before settling into a niche activity for ardent little library geeks. Bigger kids, including my older sister and brother, regarded it with amused disdain. By late July, there were only three serious contenders: me and the Horvath boys.

The Horvaths were Hungarian, refugees from the 1956 revolution. Having watched Soviet tanks occupy Budapest, the Horvaths now occupied a neat white split-level in a town a world away, where nearly everyone was Italian or Irish, the men employed as stonemasons or cops or plumbers, the women (if working) as seamstresses or secretaries.

The Horvath parents were an unprecedented partnership – *two* psychiatrists, each answering to "Doctor" in careful, faintly accented English. Dr. (Mr.) Horvath dealt with adults; Dr. (Mrs.) Horvath with children. Quiet, correct and remote, they were never joshed with, never nicknamed. But did they have glamour! All of our dads had been in the only war that mattered: The Big One, World War II. But the Horvaths had Fled Communist Oppressors. Even the nuns were impressed.

Naturally the Horvath children were top students in our Catholic school, starting with Eva, the grave-eyed daughter in my older sister's grade. Following Eva were Stephen and Ernie, who overlapped with my older brother and me. There was little noteworthy about these boys, other than the unusual precision with which they parted their hair. I hardly thought about them. In a minor way I battled Ernie academically, but unlike my older brother and his sporty gang, banes of gawky Catholic girls, Ernie was too mousy to fear. I was the class writer and Ernie was the class mathematician, which was fine with me.

❧❧

I was frankly a bit contemptuous when I first saw the Horvath boys on the wall chart. Shouldn't they be off playing with slide rules or chemistry sets? But my complacence evaporated as they attacked the contest with terrifying efficiency. Round blue stickers clustered next to their names like ants swarming a cracker crumb. Nobody else was close, just me.

And I never could catch them. Each week, I'd turn in my book list and my line of stickers would surge past the Horvaths'. But by the time I checked out another batch, they'd be back in the lead by two or three books, a pair of thoroughbreds lunging past me to the finish line.

My rage grew hot and personal. *I* never entered multiplication contests; *I* never grew bean plants for the science fair. I stayed out of their territory, so they ought to stay out of mine. It just wasn't right.

But it wasn't *inevitable*. I could restore the balance – if I dared.

❧❧

Point of fact: I didn't need two weeks to read six books. I barely needed one. I was an unnaturally fast reader.

In first grade, Sister Benedicta worried because I stammered so much as I read aloud. But this was only because my lips couldn't match the speed with which my eyes tracked. Soon enough, my reading-test scores skyrocketed. To this day, I piss people off with how fast I finish books. It's not an *accomplishment*. It's a characteristic, like nearsightedness or a flexible spine.

By third grade I was blazing through my mother's novels and my father's World War Two histories. I read at a high-school level, a secret I kept from everyone but my family and my English teachers. It was a weird skill, and I was a weird kid, with untidy dark hair and tragic square brown eyeglasses that the optician had sworn would make me look mod. Should such a girl advertise her freakish speed-reading, even to librarians? Doubtful. I always kept my books out for a decorous week, though I finished them after a day or two. Part of me reveled in my honest-to-goodness hidden power. I was a superhero in disguise.

And now, I stood alone on the contest chart against the invasion of the Horvath boys. Maybe it was time to jump from the phone booth, to plow through books faster than a speeding bullet. I might dazzle the librarians with my awe-inspiring reading rays.

Or … they might tell me to quit being a showoff, a big cheese.

A chilling thought. But the drive to win triumphed, finally. I could mop the floor with those Horvaths. I knew it. I wanted that triumphant line of stickers more than I had wanted anything before, or ever.

Yes. I would turn in those books as fast as I read them.

ॐॐ

I loved novels, but the Children's Room fiction was hopelessly babyish, an insoluble problem until I was permitted upstairs. So that summer, I dwelled among the biographies, arranged alphabetically by subject's last name in the back wall of bookcases.

I first planned to read this wall from A to Z, a project abandoned after suffering through a boringly earnest account of Jane Addams. Even after Jane, though, I hunted for stories about women, reaching beyond the lives of First Ladies swamping the shelves. I read Florence Nightingale and Louisa May Alcott, Madame Curie and Helen Keller.

I read the queens: Marie Antoinette, Mary Queen of Scots, Anne Boleyn, Elizabeth the First of England. Their dramas and dooms seized me. I spent many satisfying hours picturing the details, if not the actual deed, of my own execution: my heavy robes, my stately walk, my stirring speech, the keepsakes I would distribute among my loyal followers. I was splendid at comforting distraught ladies-in-waiting.

∂∽∂

By the day I prowled the stacks, primed to fire my secret weapon, I'd already read most of the good biographies. Gritting my teeth, I added Martha Washington, Dolley Madison and Mary Todd Lincoln to my pile. I bumped my total to six with a trio of women whose fame had faded like the ink on their out-of-print lives: Narcissa Whitman, Dorothea Dix, Edith Cavell.

At checkout, the librarian smiled indulgently at my pile of nonfiction. Let's call her Mrs. McGoff, petite and pale-lipsticked, with auburn hair lacquered into an up-do. The dark-pink frames of her eyeglasses tilted delicately upward, a pair of rose-colored butterflies.

From her file drawer, Mrs. McGoff extracted my dog-eared card with its silver metal strip embedded at the bottom. Setting it across the bed of the heavy imprinting machine, she began the familiar, soothing dance of checkout – pulling out the pocket card, imprinting my name and the due date, replacing the card and closing the cover.

Turn-flip-slip-stack-click/whoosh-shut. Six times.

"Thank you," I dared to whisper.

"You're welcome," she whispered back. "I'll see you soon, I'm sure."

I risked a tiny smile in return and hurried out, glancing at the chart by the door. The Horvaths were ahead, as usual.

Not for long, I thought.

☙❧

I read like a demon, forgoing snacks and sleep and bike rides, reddening my eyes. My mother told me to go outside and get some fresh air. I ignored her. I do not remember how long I waited before speeding back on my bike to the library. It was definitely less than a week; maybe only two days.

(Maybe, oh, just maybe, I had the gall to go back on the very next day.)

☙❧

My hand shook with excitement as I filled out my contest slip. Possibilities gleamed, dazzling as the fluorescent ceiling lights. They'd have to expand the chart to contain my overflowing stickers. Jealous kids would marvel. The librarians would shake my hand. And best of all was picturing how I would treat the Horvaths.

I might be dignified, gracious in victory like Madame Curie picking up her Nobel Prizes. I'd tell the Horvaths they mustn't get discouraged.

(*Life is not easy for any of us*, Madame Curie once said. *But what of that? We must have perseverance, and above all, confidence in ourselves.*)

Or, I might be Elizabeth the First, fierce and unabashed. I might tell the Horvaths that justice had finally overtaken them, the invaders, the showoffs.

(*Let tyrants fear!* shouted Elizabeth, the Spanish Armada bobbing at her back.)

Winning was inevitable; it was only a question of style.

❧⟡

Mrs. McGoff's eyebrows shot past her rose-colored frames when I deposited my contest slip on her desk, but she said nothing. Probably she was saving her praise for checkout time.

I was far too excited about picking out my next six books to think much about it. Diving into the biographies, I grabbed another trio of First Ladies: Lou Henry Hoover, Eleanor Roosevelt, Jacqueline Kennedy. Now, who else? Well, I hadn't done Amelia Earhart yet. I pivoted and swept toward Subjects, Biographical, D to E, scanning the spines anxiously. Was Amelia checked out?

The back wall of biographies was my kingdom, screened from the rest of the room by the stacks. I glanced down the aisles occasionally, on alert for rowdy boys or annoying little kids, but nobody appeared. On this golden day, the Children's Room held the peace of a churchyard.

I nabbed Earhart, Amelia. There were four books on my arm, and two more to go. Pausing at an aisle, I peeked over at the librarians' desk, and saw that Mrs. McGoff was no longer alone. She was talking to the Children's Room boss.

The Children's Room Boss was dark and fierce. I never knew her name; I wouldn't have asked her anything, not even where the fire exit was. She typed ferociously in a tiny cubicle behind the front desk, and only checked books out if there was a line five deep at the counter, when she stepped in with an air of scornful martyrdom. Strange to see her at the counter when there was no line.

And *whispering*.

The weirdness of this whispering makes little sense today, when you can meet for coffee at a library, or run a study group. But in the libraries of my childhood, silence was a sacrament, settling its weight upon your shoulders as soon the door shut behind you. Even librarians were silent unless absolutely necessary, resorting to a librarian mime-language of shrugs, nods and finger-taps.

Yet here were two librarians, whispering. Why?

సారా

OK. I had to get two more books, check out, and go home. I already could feel my hands closing around the sparkly blue grips of my Schwinn, feel my feet pressing the trusty pedals.

At the front desk, they still whispered. Mrs. McGoff glanced up; saw me staring, looked sharply away. I shrank back into the biographies, something small and sick writhing in my stomach. My hand grazed the Ds and struck out blindly, grabbing a life of Lee DeForest. *Lee DeForest?* Who was he? Who cared? One more book to go.

My ears strained toward the front desk. The murmurs were maddeningly indistinct, distant as the whine of the trucks on Route 22 that lulled me to sleep at night.

Suddenly, the silence returned. I could hear my breathing, too loud, too fast. Slowing it with an effort, I tried to study the spines of the Ds.

A hand closed lightly around my elbow. Only strict training stopped me from yelping.

"Hello," said Mrs. McGoff, unsmiling. "What are you reading this week?"

Wordlessly, I displayed my armload.

Mrs. McGoff picked up the Lee DeForest book I'd grabbed in a panic. "This looks easy to read," she said, studying the blurb on the back cover. "Hmm. Only a fifth-grade book? You mustn't read below your grade level. What grade are you in?"

"I just finished third. I start fourth grade in the fall," I whispered. (Was I permitted to speak any louder?)

"Still." She returned Lee DeForest to me. "You must choose books that are more difficult. A little more of a challenge."

"OK," I whispered. "I'll try."

And Mrs. McGoff meandered away as if librarians always talked to kids this way.

Did they?

అ~ఆ

I thought: I should just check out and go. I could get that sixth book later. The problem was that now, the front desk was deserted. I paced the aisles, pondering.

I could go up front, slam my books down, look impatient. But that only worked for adults. Well, maybe I could call out: "Excuse me!" But … out *loud*? In the *library*? Was I nuts?

Maybe I could just take the books and run.

It never occurred to me to leave the books behind.

⌘

When Mrs. McGoff found me again, I was 80 percent panicked but still 20 percent mystified.

"Come with me, dear," she said. We strode toward the wall with the conference-room door and the water fountain. It was a relief to have a directive, a destination. Perhaps Mrs. McGoff needed a drink of water? No. She was opening the dark walnut door to a room I had never seen unlocked or lit.

In fact, I had never personally known anyone who had been in that conference room, until me.

I remember a table, long and narrow. I remember the Children's Boss sitting there, black-browed and cool-eyed, with a tall young woman I couldn't quite place, her expression calm, her brown hair clipped by a tortoiseshell barrette. Who was she? Realization hit with a shock: the remembered sight of her through the main lobby's glass doors, behind a bigger circulation desk.

She was from the Adult Room!

They had brought an *Adult Room librarian* down here to talk to me. And in front of her, neatly stacked, were the books I had returned that morning.

⌘

Mrs. McGoff sat to the left of the Adult Room librarian, with the Children's Boss on the right. They waved me to a seat across from them. The pile of books loomed between us.

"Don't be afraid," said the Adult Room librarian.

Yes, I thought. A queen must face her enemies fearlessly, her shoulders back, her gaze fierce. I managed this for about five seconds. I was no brave, doomed queen – I was the sniveling informant who would throw six queens under the bus to save my miserable skin, before the thumbscrews even started twisting.

The Adult Room librarian sensed my terror, as a good inquisitor should. She smiled. "We just – "

"We need you to answer a few questions," the Children's Boss cut in.

One look from the Adult Room librarian, and the Children's Boss shut up. (Even in my panic, I admired this effortless pulling of rank.) Sliding the books closer, the Adult Room librarian glanced through them as if she might want to check one out for herself. She picked up a thick volume bound in an ugly, muddy gray.

"Can you tell me about this one?" asked the Adult Room lady. She was holding the Edith Cavell biography. "What is this about?"

"Well." I swallowed. "It's … about Edith Cavell."

Three pairs of eyes pinned mine from across the table.

"And who was she?" asked the Adult Room lady, kindly.

"She, uh, she was English. A nurse."

The Adult Room librarian cocked her head, alert, interested. I fell for it, probably as intended. I liked to talk about what I read, and I rarely was invited to do it.

(*Big cheese! Showoff!*)

I said: "Well, she was in Belgium during World War One …"

The eyes across the table never wavered from my face, as I talked about my books.

❧❦

They never explained what was happening, or why. Sometimes my mouth felt dry, and I wished I could step outside to the water fountain, but no one suggested we take a break. Once, I stopped summarizing to say anxiously, "I did read the books," hating myself instantly for sucking up. But nobody answered; maybe they didn't hear.

They sent me back into the Children's Room when they were done. Alone again, I thought the bookcases seemed taller; the ceiling pressed down lower. I turned away from the contest chart by the door and shuffled back to my wall of biographies. My every nerve sang and tingled, on red alert. (For what?)

Part of me still saw those eyes staring at me across that table. This part wanted to sob and hit things, to run out of the library. But another part of me was hanging tough. Maybe this was all a test to see what a brilliant reader looked like. A *good* test. The librarians might be figuring out how best to – what had Mrs. McGoff said? To *challenge* me. Yes.

The conference-room door clicked open. Soft footfalls plodded toward the front desk. I risked a peek through the stacks and saw Mrs. McGoff looking at her blotter, fiddling with a pen.

I tried hard not to *trot* to her. But I did so want to go home. I wanted to lose myself in my books, this week, the week after that, and forever. To read and read until the books had smothered every whisper, every question of this morning. I might even have succeeded – that's just how much I loved to read.

However: Mrs. McGoff had left the conference-room door ajar, and as I walked by, I heard the other two librarians.

"But – returning them so soon." The Children's Room Boss sounded peevish. "I do *not* feel right about this."

"She appears to have read the books," the Adult Room librarian said briskly. "I don't know what exactly it is you want me to *do* – "

I stumbled on.

At the front desk, Mrs. McGoff checked out my books. "Only five?" she asked, brightly. I said nothing. The verdict still hissed in my ears: *Appears to have read.*

Not *obviously.* Not *definitely.*

They did not think I was a brilliant reader. They weren't even sure I was a *real* reader. They thought I might have cheated.

There it was: My axe, my guillotine blade.

Turn-flip-slip-stack-click/whoosh-shut.

❧

Back home, my older brother and sister needled me into telling them what was up. When I finally cracked, they surprised me.

"That's bogus," said my brother – the merciless teaser who stole my diary and pranced around the house with it, delivering dramatic readings. "They're not giving the Horvaths a hard time and look how many books *they* return."

"Totally unfair," said my older sister, who considered me mortifying by virtue of breathing.

We agreed that we would not tell the younger kids; they had nothing useful to add. But should we tell our parents? Now *there* was a question. How could we classify what happened at the library? It hovered uncertainly between punishment and reward, the two established categories of adult dealings. This was the 1960s of peace, love and rock 'n' roll, but this was also my parents' house, where nobody was marching and nothing was free.

My father rarely believed there were two sides to any story – if there'd been another side, there wouldn't have *been* a story. And though our mother acknowledged the unfairness periodically doled out by teachers (or librarians), she did not believe in contesting it. If every parent whined about settled decisions, the world would soon go to hell in a handbasket. You shouldn't fight City Hall.

We decided to say nothing, and hope the librarians wouldn't phone home.

৵৹৵

"I wonder if the *Horvaths* ever got called in," my older brother said, darkly.

I hunched a shoulder, not wanting to talk about it. But I wondered, too.

Supposing they *had* called the Horvaths into the conference room. So what? The Drs. Horvath, who once faced down Communist tanks, could easily have faced down the Children's Boss – the Adult Room lady, even. That's what must have happened.

Unless … perhaps they never did call the Horvaths in. Perhaps they simply believed that the Horvath boys were brilliant readers, real readers – just as they believed I was a fake.

৵৹৵

The librarians never called. The contest went on.

For the rest of that summer, I pedaled to the library only when a little kid whined for a big kid to go along. I checked out four or five books, never six, always making sure they were above fifth-grade level. I waited two weeks before returning anything.

I still filled out contest slips, fearing questions if I suddenly stopped. But I never looked at the chart on the wall.

My mother was puzzled that I'd stopped chattering about the library contest, but asked no questions. And an elderly cousin visiting in August from Long Island said she was glad to see me playing tag and dolls for once, like a real girl.

৵৽৽

Suddenly, Labor Day was around the corner.

My older brother's gang squeezed every possible second from their dwindling supply of vacation, pushing sandlot games deep into the twilight over their mothers' insistent calls to supper. I tried on my new school uniform and made sure my pencil case was fully restocked. When my older sister brought the certificate home from the library, I was honestly surprised.

"You still finished second," she said.

I had read eighty-three books that summer – more than anyone except the Horvath boys, whose totals tied, so they both got blue ribbons.

I got a red ribbon.

The certificate stayed tucked into a green leatherette corner of the blotter on my desk, in the attic bedroom I shared with my two youngest sisters. It wasn't an honor and it wasn't a keepsake. I'd have torn it up, except I didn't have the authority to destroy official documents. The red ribbon made me queasy. It proclaimed my secret power as a secret disgrace – grounds for interrogation, not a ticker-tape parade.

৵৽৽

My father's oldest sister had the last word, as usual. Aunt Catherine was famous for never backing down from an argument, never being impressed and never sparing feelings in doing a kindness. ("Here. I thought yiz needed some bath towels," she once told my mother, thrusting a Macy's bag at her. "Yours are frayed.")

One autumn weekend, Aunt Catherine trekked to our house via subway and bus from Brooklyn. After exclaiming our thanks for the usual boxes of Devil Dogs from Drake's Cakes, her employer, we kids prepared to scram. But then our aunt asked us what was new. Nobody could think of anything. She tended to blank our minds like that.

"Elizabeth won a prize," blurted one of the little kids.

"No, I *didn't*, stupid," I said. (Little kids. Why did God make them?)

"You did! From the library."

"You don't say," Aunt Catherine said.

"It wasn't much." I looked at the floor. "It's dumb."

"E-*liz*-a-beth!" My mother glared at me. "Go get your certificate to show your aunt."

"Mom – "

"*Go.*"

All too soon I was dragging my way toward my aunt, the certificate held behind my back.

"So? Let's see it."

I handed it over. "I *told* you," I said. "I only got a red ribbon."

Aunt Catherine ignored this. Through her round, wire-rimmed spectacles, she looked at the paper in her hand, then back at me.

"My God, Elizabeth Anne," she said. "Eighty-three books! God love you."

When people like my aunt said "God love you," it might mean you were a complete idiot. But it might also mean you were sort of an ace.

My aunt's expression implied that she actually thought I was an ace.

"Eighty-three books," Aunt Catherine said again, running her thumb across the blood-red ribbon pasted on the certificate. "I don't think I've read eighty-three books in my *life*. That's something, Elizabeth Anne! That's really something."

My Aunt Catherine said that, when I was nine years old. Which is why the certificate has stayed with me through relocations to four states, through hasty packing jobs in sloppy boxes, through short-term leases and long-term mortgages.

I still don't know whether the librarians ever believed what they typed on that certificate. But Aunt Catherine, the toughest of tough birds, believed what she read on it. So do I, now. Those eighty-three books *were* really something.

More important, they were something real.

As real as anything can be.

Honorable Mention - Alphabetic Order
Ruth Rudner
New Mexico

Ruth Rudner began exploring the Alps while living in Austria, writing for Ski Magazine. In the course of summers spent hiking from hut to hut and learning to rock climb, she encountered the words on the wall that inspired *The Courage of Cowards*, and that remain for her a necessary mantra. Returning to the U.S., she continued writing about mountains, wildlife, and nature in general. For many years a frequent contributor to the *Wall St. Journal* Leisure & Arts Page, she is the author of four books of personal essays and is currently working on a novel.

Ruth Rudner

The Courage of Cowards

Nur Mut, Johann, someone had painted on the rock wall. "Only courage, Johann."

The writing, a bit above where I rested partway up my climb of the wall, appeared at exactly the right time. The next move required letting go of the secure ledge on which I stood to leap upward over a small crack, aiming for a ledge some inches above to the right. It was the only way to get there. The ledge was not far, but letting go to jump upward scared the hell out of me.

Obviously, Johann had felt the same way. A kind friend of his had gone ahead to encourage him; to let him know the doing of this thing only required courage. That Johann had the skill to make the jump goes without saying, or he wouldn't have gotten this high on the *Gimpelwesgrat* in the first place. That was true of me as well.

But I am afraid of things. *Summoning* courage may be the only way I can make it up the mountain, across the stream, into a crowded room, through the day, through whatever scares me. Calling upon it often, courage has become a familiar, a trusted teacher. Familiar, but not automatic. Rarely my immediate response, it is my fallback, the thing that happens after searching for the coward's way out.

Once, on a NY subway, when a fire broke out between cars, people began screaming, rushing toward the far end of the car, past where, seeing the fire, I hung for dear life onto a pole in front of the door. I hung on because I did not want to become part of the rush, did not want to join the crowd where, it seemed to me, if we were not killed by the fire, we would be trampled. With every instinct telling me to move as far from the fire as I could, as fast as I could, I forced myself to hang on. Tightening my grip, I insisted to my fear that I stay where I was.

The train inched into the station, opened its doors. I clutched the pole while people ran out. I walked out. I walked up the subway platform, up the steps. I came to the street where the sky was clear and no one knew what had happened underground.

Hanging on in the face of panic rising is an old feeling. I have felt it most of my life. For me that amounts to courage, the ability to remain at least outwardly still in the face of apparent danger.

For cowards, opportunities for this practice are rife.

In the Dolomites, there are trails known as *Via Ferrata*. They are trails with aids—iron ropes or ladders-- nailed into the rock to help one through and up and over difficult landscapes --sheer cliffs, narrow rock ledges, unhikable mountains. This is climbers' terrain. Except it isn't. Once, after hiking the *Sentiero Bonacossa* from the *Rifugio Auronzo* to the *Rifugio Fratelli Fonda Savio* in the *Dolomiti di Sesto*, I was told about a woman on the same trail earlier in the season. Her husband was behind her on the trail where, only a few inches wide, it passes beneath a low overhang, requiring one to walk bent forward. On the exposed side there is a long drop down sheer rock to the valley. The husband noticed something interesting. He called to his wife. "Rita . . . ."

"Yes," she said, turning to answer and instantly falling to her death, pushed over the side by her pack hitting the overhang.

158

If I had known before I did that trail, would I have gone? Probably. It was the route from the place I was to the place I was going. Would I have been terrified? Maybe. In the face of that, would it have been courageous or foolhardy to go? Or neither. Just necessity. Just the route from one place to another.

Is that what courage is? The willingness to get from one place to another? The willingness to move through any perceived danger and come out the other side? From this side of the mountain to the other. From this belief to its opposite. From this struggle to its resolution. Is it the same for the fearless, the adrenaline addicts who do not hesitate to sky dive or hang glide, to ride monster waves, race cars, walk tightropes without a safety net? It always seemed to me the physically fearless have no need of courage. The fearless simply do the thing they're doing. But what happens when they must sit quietly and alone; when they are asked to meditate, to contemplate? Is this frightening? Does this also require courage? Is courage the means for doing something the opposite of our nature? Or does it simply mean putting oneself at risk for some greater good? Does the word "courage" only apply when the motive is unselfish?

Hiking in the Brenta Range, enroute from the *Rifugio Silvio Agostini* to the *Rifugio Dodici Apostoli*, my husband and I found our path obstructed by a 656 foot high wall. Rather, our path simply changed its geometry from horizontal to vertical. Sixteen ladders scale the wall, the ladders held in place by nails pounded through the rails at top and bottom. On the small ledges between the top of one ladder and the bottom of the next, iron cable secures the way. The ladders hug the wall, with no space to commit a foot too far onto a rung, and little space to wrap your fingers. You cannot linger on a rung.

Behind you there is nothing but space. To either side, there is nothing but space. Only in front of you do you get the comfort of secure earth. Rock solid vertical earth. A thing on which to focus.

You learn early in climbing not to look down, not to look out. You learn to focus. Focused, it is the thing itself, the thing on which you focus, that takes your attention, and not the dangers surrounding the thing, not the peripheral, not the irrelevant. Keep your attention of the thing itself, and you will survive.

Yet, knowing this, the lure to look elsewhere is huge. You want to see what will happen if you do; you want to check out whether or not this ability to focus is all it's cracked up to be. So you must fight that. You must force yourself into the focus. You must only do what is there in front of you to do. Are focus and courage the same word?

My husband climbed first. I waited until he had exited the first ladder to begin my own climb. He was soon out of my view. The first ladders were straightforward enough, although climbing them took its toll on my arm strength. Nearing the top, as the ladders became longer, my arms became tired. I felt my rucksack as a pull backward. There was no way to adjust it as I climbed. There was no way to adjust it anyway. It was just there. As the tops of ladders seemed further and further away, I longed for the safety of horizontal ground. But there were only the ledges, the steps to the next ladder, the climb, one rung at a time. I was ready for an end.

The right-hand rail of the last ladder had lost its bottom nail sending the ladder on a slight swing out into space on that side. It seemed securely held on the left-hand rail. I prayed it still held at the top. I prayed as I stepped onto the bottom rung, my weight forcing the ladder into a greater swing toward the left, the swing emphasized by the weight of my pack. Here, more than on any of the other ladders, here, where my arms were most tired, it was the most necessary to hold on by the strength of my arms. By the strength of my will. By the will of God. In the ladder's swing, movement upward required yet more strength than I had yet needed. I had two options; continue up in the face of my mounting fear, or back my way down, first step off this ladder swinging outward, then all the ladders I had already surmounted. And then what? Where would I go? My husband was at the top of this wall. The *Rifugio Dodici Apostoli* required getting to the top of this wall. In fact, I had no options. I could not go down. I stepped onto the second rung. The swing increased. Focus. I forced my mind onto the rock holding the ladder. I prayed. I climbed. I ached. I longed for the top. I tried not to wonder what the fall would feel like. 656 feet. Almost 656 feet. It was 656 feet from the top, and I was not yet there. I moved my hands, one at a time to the next rung and the next. I lifted each foot. Heavily, I lifted each foot. There was my husband. I was at the top.

"I didn't think you would be able to do it," he said.

"There was no choice," I said, shaking, lying on the rock of the top, grateful, terrified, finally able to give in to my terror.

Was I courageous? I doubt it. Is courage involved when there is no choice?

My first book was about mountain hiking in the Alps. On a few pages devoted to "Wandering for Cowards," I wrote, "Coming to a steep pass or a narrow ledge or anything else that might make you a little afraid, you know you have only to walk through your fear. Once on the other side of the pass you are on the other side of the fear. Your confidence and skill have been increased and the next time you are not afraid. When it is really necessary to turn back it is common sense, not cowardice, that makes the decision. The most important thing for cowards to remember is that they are the only people who are truly brave. The fearless have no need of courage."

Seventeen years later I sat in on a book group talking about a book I had just published, a collection of essays about my move from New York to Montana. But wanting to hear genuine reactions to the book, I was there incognito. Most of the all-women group were complimentary, getting involved in the adventure of the essays. One woman, however, did not like the book. She felt the author spent too much time dealing with fear.

She was the one who got it right. Yes, there was adventure in that book. And yes, every single adventure involved dealing with fear. I doubt I was aware of that as I wrote. It wasn't until the woman spoke that I understood it; that I understood I had probably spent my entire life dealing with fear.

It makes no sense to me. My parents never presented fear to me. When my mother was a very old woman she told me she was afraid of lightning. "Since when?" I asked. "Always," she said. But once, when I was a small child watching a storm, frightened of the sound of thunder, the flash of lightning, she told me that the lightning was so animals could see their way to shelter. We watched the lightning together as I imagined rabbits running for their holes, bears for their dens. Could I have felt her fear in spite of her brave insistence she would not transfer it to me?

Is it appropriate to write an essay about courage from the point of view of fear? Or is that what is exactly right?

When I was two years old, my father, an expert rider who had grown up on horseback, put me on a horse. Terrified, I cried to be lifted down. I remember the feeling. The horse was so big. I was so little. I was so far from the ground. My father, unwilling to allow me to be frightened, lifted me down.

It took me forty-four years to get back on.

Through all that time, I loved horses. I found them beautiful. I longed to be a part of the horse's world. I longed to ride forever into the sunset on my wild-maned horse. But I was too frightened to even lean over a fence and pat a horse.

At forty-six, newly at home in Montana, it seemed to be time. I registered for beginning equitation at Montana State University. At the first class I explained to the instructor, the head of the animal husbandry department, that I was terrified of horses. "I'll give you Babs Barmaid," he said. "She's a special for cowards."

Twice a week I drove to the equestrian center for my class, me and eleven twenty-year olds. I watched the instructor intensely, copied his every move. Or, attempted to. A young Crow Indian woman adopted me. Although she had been riding her entire life, she was taking the class because she had had no formal training. She would learn by teaching me. I would learn because I refused to fail. I would learn because I had a guide.

I surprised the instructor with my ability in the final exam, but took the class a second time to increase my confidence. Fine in the arena, I was uneasy when we took the horses outside. "Horses belong outside," I told myself every time we moved through the doorway, wishing the instructor would change his mind and we could return to the arena. Still, the second time worked like a charm. Babs Barmaid and I knew how to work together. I went on to the intermediate class. I participated in a five day horsepacking trip in Yellowstone, starting, of course, by telling the outfitter that I was a coward.

"I have just the horse for you," he said. "Pepper can read any rider. She'll take care of a beginner, or rodeo if you want to."

I rode Pepper on several trips with that outfitter, eventually going to work with him, loading mules, pulling a train of mules over the miles of Yellowstone wilderness, driving a truck too big for me pulling a 12-horse trailer, teaching the tourists who came on the trips to saddle and bridle their horses, to ride the Yellowstone trails. I was no longer afraid. Sometimes people commented on how brave I was to be doing some of the things I was doing. I no longer thought of myself as a coward. I was doing work I loved. And did well.

Courage is the most personal thing we possess. Rumi writes, "The only thing we possess is that which we will not lose in a shipwreck." Courage. Maybe. *Nur mut, Johann*

Via television, the internet, newspapers, magazine articles, I see how people behave in the face of grave danger. How bravely people behave. I do not believe these people are fearless. I believe they are people like me, sometimes opting for work that puts them in the danger zones of the world, meeting it head on, committed to the work. Sometimes simply dealing with the fate of their lives. Sometimes dealing with the necessity for change. It requires courage to get up in the morning and do the thing that scares you. It is courage that allows you to walk through fear.

My husband (who by the time of my move to Montana was no longer my husband) once said that if I was afraid of something, I would simply go out and do it, that it seemed to be the only way I knew to deal with fear. In this way, the lines I wrote in my first book about wandering for cowards remain correct, even though, as I reread them, I have to wonder at how flip it's possible to be when you are young. With the physical skill to do anything, you can afford to talk about being a coward, and therefore being brave.

Is it the same from this side of my life?